Praise for *How to Hire A-Players*

"The definitive book on talent acquisition, *How To Hire A-Players* pulls no punches. From the get-go, Eric Herrenkohl strongly recommends that organizations stop trying to turn poor performers into top performers. The goal is to commit more time to finding and hiring the best talent. This initiative begins by recruiting the team you need rather than settling for the team you have. In a well-written masterpiece, Eric emphatically concludes that what organizations need is a perfect storm: hire individuals with terrific communication skills, great project management skills, detail orientation, intelligence, and responsibility. This kind of talent will create shock value for an organization. Organizations are very much like most living organisms, they are likely to expire quickly if the vital organs are not taken care of. This book offers precise, almost surgical, advice on how to ensure that the vital organs of any organization, its people, are the strongest possible. These valuable assets will enable its existence and assure that it continually thrives.

This book is full of anecdotes that truly reflect the importance of due diligence in finding and retaining A-players. This is an important read that will pay huge dividends for your organization. I believe it is the definitive book on talent acquisition in recent memory and a cogent blueprint for all organizations."

—Benjamin Ola Akande, PhD
Dean, School of Business and Technology
Webster University

"This is a book about business and how recruiting relates to winning. Eric has brought to life how hiring A-players can make you an A-player as a leader or business owner. His system is simple to understand and natural to utilize. With it, you have an immediate leg up on the competition."

—Chris Burkhard
President
CBI Group

"Consistently hiring A-players takes a lot more than just a good job description. You have to have a *system* for finding, hiring, and keeping great people, and Eric Herrenkohl's process sets the foundation for hiring only the best candidates."

—Diane Butrus
Chief Operating Officer
Bronx/Diba/Luichiny Shoes

"As an information technology executive in the food services industry, I am convinced that A-Players are critical to compete and to deliver high quality outcomes to our clients. Eric Herrenkohl has managed to create a 'cook book' for creating A-player teams. This book offers a step-by-step 'recipes'-style approach that helps non-HR leaders create high performing teams, while encouraging improvement through clarity of roles throughout the entire organization."

—Lawrence Dillon
VP/CIO
ARAMARK Healthcare

"Herrenkohl provides an entertaining and comprehensive approach to building the backbone of every company. Through real life stories, Herrenkohl masterfully uncovers the approach and the mind-set required to deliver sustainable performance improvements in your organization through recruiting, developing, and retaining top talent. Integrate this advice into your management systems and unleash the true potential of your business!"

—Al D'Iorio
Chief Financial Officer
Swiss Farms Stores Acquisition, LLC

"Building successful start-ups is all about winning the war for 'A' talent. The concept is simple. 'A' players attract other 'A' players while 'B' players attract 'C' players. You'd be well advised to put into practice Eric's philosophy and approach on attracting 'A' talent which mirrors many of the practices I have seen work in the leading Silicon Valley companies."

—Jason Green
General Partner
Emergence Capital

"Great stuff—especially right now. This is not just another fluff business book telling us what we already know but can't execute. Eric has pulled together a comprehensive, *practical* but more importantly *implementable* process that every CEO or owner of a growing business should use. If you're interested in not just growing, but growing smartly and profitably, *and* building a fabulous team that will get you there, Eric's book is a must-read."

—Cheryl Beth Kuchler
Founder and Managing Principal
CEO Think Tank

"Before I started my business, a businessman I greatly respect counseled me that I would never be able to attract A-players. It made sense to him because third-tier subcontractors don't usually attract the best and the brightest. Yet working with Eric and his principles, and believing in what we offer to the best people, has led to an entire team of A-players and more success than we could have imagined."

—Rich Ledbetter
President
Castle Contracting

"*How to Hire A-Players* is a must for anyone in the business world who is looking for a recruiting system which addresses the fundamental concepts of how to recognize and acquire top talent in the workforce. This practical how-to guide is for business leaders who are seeking high caliber players to take them to the next level."

—Mark Neal
Managing Partner
Milhouse & Neal, LLP

"Whether you lead a small team or large organization, you know that great teams consist of great people, but do you know how to find them? *How to Hire A-Players* shows you how to build your talent pipeline and recruit the A-players you need to deliver the results you want. Eric Herrenkohl delivers a straightforward and powerful message drawing on his experience coaching and consulting A-players. He's nailed it."

—Mark Peterman
Vice President, Performance Solutions
Staples Promotional Products

"Under the hood of every company that has excelled and risen to dominate in its industry, you will find a team of A-players. *How to Hire A-Players* is a definitive and tactical arsenal of tools and strategies that a business needs to assemble and retain such a team and take itself to these levels."

—Josh Peterson
Founder, Adteractive Active Entrepreneur,
Angel Investor, Start-up Advisor

"Not only does Eric remind you that recruiting is an A-1 important function in your business, he has written a book that gives you the 'how to' for building a team of A-players. Read this book—you will learn how to build a successful organization."

—Maryann Vitale
Managing Broker/Owner
Prudential Select Properties

"Everyone talks talent, but very few know where to find it. Eric Herrenkohl has created the ultimate executive playbook for how to recruit and build the team you need. *How to Hire A-Players* is just like Eric's coaching . . . comprehensive yet succinct, practical, and immediately actionable. I wish I'd had this book five years ago."

—Michael J. Weinberg
Senior Vice President, Sales
The Gabriel Group

HOW
TO HIRE
A-PLAYERS

HOW TO HIRE
A-PLAYERS

Finding the Top People for Your Team—Even If You Don't Have a Recruiting Department

Eric Herrenkohl

WILEY

John Wiley & Sons, Inc.

Published by John Wiley & Sons, Inc., Hoboken, New Jersey.

Published simultaneously in Canada.

For general information on our other products and services or for technical support, please contact our Customer Care Department within the United States at (800) 762-2974, outside the United States at (317) 572-3993 or fax (317) 572-4002.

Wiley also publishes its books in a variety of electronic formats. Some content that appears in print may not be available in electronic books. For more information about Wiley products, visit our web site at www.wiley.com.

Library of Congress Cataloging-in-Publication Data:

Herrenkohl, Eric, 1967-
   How to hire A-players: finding the top people for your team—even if you don't have a recruiting department/Eric Herrenkohl.
      p. cm.
   ISBN 978-0-470-56224-6 (cloth)
   e-ISBNs 978-0-470-618-54-7, 978-0-470-618-66-0, 978-0-470-618-67-7
   1.   Employee selection. 2.   Employees–Recruiting. I.   Title.
   HF5549.5.S38H478 2010
   658.3'11—dc22

                                                    2009046302

Printed in the United States of America.

10 9 8 7 6 5 4 3 2 1

*To my parents, Roy Herrenkohl
and Ellen Herrenkohl*

*Thank you for loving your sons and
teaching us to love learning*

Contents

Acknowledgments

A number of people have been of great help to me in writing this book. It would be impossible to thank everyone who has done so, but I would like to highlight a few folks for special commendation.

First of all, I wouldn't have anything to say if I didn't have the privilege of working with great clients who lead terrific businesses. I appreciate the chance to add value to your organizations and to get to know you in the process. Thank you for sharing your stories with my readers—we can all learn from your experiences.

Paul Van De Putte introduced me to my agent Kirk Schroder, Managing Partner of Schroder Fidlow & Titley, PLC in Richmond, Va. Paul, I appreciate the introduction. Thanks for being the kind of person that everyone wants to know and for your friendship. Kirk, this book would not have happened without your work on my behalf. Thank you.

I want to thank my friend Bob Perkins for his wisdom on "leading leaders," which has shaped my own thinking about how to attract and keep A-players. Thanks also to my friend and mentor Walter Green for your time, your interest in me, and for teaching me always to ask and answer the question, "What does success look like?"

Dan Ambrosio, my editor at John Wiley & Sons, Inc., was the person who gave me a shot to publish this book commercially. Thank you, Dan! Thanks also to Christine Moore, Kate Lindsay, and Ashley Allison at Wiley, who did a terrific job of tightening up the writing in this book and making it commercial grade.

Thanks to the many people who took time out of their busy schedules to provide me with their perspective on how to hire A-players, including: Megan Bittle, Tim Bradley, Chris Burkhard,

Vita Burdi, Diane Butrus, Colin Drummond, Carl Gersbach, Jay Gettis, Todd Gibson, Rob Gilfillan, Lulu Gonella, Ed and Ellen Griffin, Vic Haas, Verne Harnish, Dave Hartman, Jody and Heather Herzog, Rob Holiday, Elaine Hughes, Greg Hutchings, Barney Kister, Rich Ledbetter, Brad Lyons, Tom McKendry, Tom McShane, Tracy Moore, Mark Peterman, Jeff Phillips, Tyler Ridgeway, Shirley Ann Rizi, Rich Ryffel, Steve Schultz, Barbie Spear, David Spetnagel, Suzanne Taylor, Sam Toumayan, Paul Van De Putte, Mike Vaughan, Karyn Verrett, Tony Vice, Maryann Vitale, and Mike Weiss. Special thanks to Fred Christen for his perspective on building a farm team; to Justin Smith for multiple cell-phone calls about using recruiters wisely; to Matt Todt for his insight on managing recruiters; to Ryan Lafferty for his time, expertise, and for breakfast; and to Tracy Cote and Traci Armstrong for sharing their experiences with recruiting via Twitter.

Thank you very much to Joe Kearfott and Ellen Herrenkohl for reviewing and editing the page proofs of this book—I appreciated it.

Finally, I have an unfair advantage in all of life, including writing a book, because of the woman to whom I am married. Kelly read, edited, and greatly improved everything about this book, from the initial proposal to the final manuscript. Smart, fun, and good looking is a great combination in someone with whom you get to spend your life. Thanks for everything.

—Eric Herrenkohl
Philadelphia, PA

About the Author

Eric Herrenkohl is the founder and president of Herrenkohl Consulting (www.herrenkohlconsulting.com), which helps executives create the businesses they want by building the organizations they need. Herrenkohl Consulting's client list includes privately-held businesses across fifty industries as well as a number of Fortune and Service 500 companies. Eric is an expert author for Monster. com and has been featured by Fox News, the *Philadelphia Inquirer*, Inc.com, and MSNBC.com. He serves as a keynote speaker for business and professional groups and is the author of "Performance Principles," a highly-regarded e-letter that brings strategies for building businesses to readers around the globe. He lives with his wife and four children in the greater Philadelphia area.

Introduction: Where Do I Find Great People?

"Eric, where do I find great people?"

This is the question clients ask me more often than any other. "Sure, sure," they say, "I know we should interview more and be willing to train extensively. But how do I find great people in the first place?"

I wrote this book to provide an answer, once and for all, to that question. It is an executive's playbook written for busy managers who want strategies and tactics for building a team of A-players.

What's my definition of an A-player? An A-player is an employee who creates superior results compared to the vast majority of other people who hold the same position in your industry. If you want to build an A-player team, you need to stop trying to turn poor performers into top performers and commit more time to finding and hiring A-players. Then, invest the same leadership and coaching time with them that you used to spend trying to fix your poor performers. You will be amazed at the measurable improvement in results that you see.

Here's just one example of what one A-player can do for a company. Alex and James, principals at an architectural firm, hired me to help improve sales results and staff productivity. Through a lot of intensive work, we freed up Alex and James to sell more business, got the senior architects below them effectively managing projects, and helped the project architects to develop the skills they needed to run their own projects without much handholding. It was a lot of work, but it paid off. The architects improved, and the firm got more productive.

However, there were still a few architects in the firm who just could not get up to speed and who didn't seem to have the skills or the drive to improve their performance. That's where we made our mistake. We spent a lot of time (months and months) trying to get these people to improve their performance. They made very limited progress.

In the midst of this, the firm hired a young architect named Tim, a perfect storm of terrific communication skills, great project management skills, good detail orientation, intelligence, and responsibility. After just a couple of years, clients were asking to work with him.

Not only was Tim naturally talented, he flourished in the leadership coaching program that we had established. We set goals for him, and he met them. We provided him with coaching on specific skills, he quickly absorbed and used the new knowledge. We put a career plan in place for him, and he aggressively put in the effort to move to the next level in the firm.

This experience—and others like it—taught me that businesses that want to thrive must always be on the lookout for their next "Tim." An organization's owners, managers, and employees must commit to finding A-players whenever and wherever they can. If recruiting remains a necessary evil for your company, you will never build an A-player team. However, if you're dedicated to building a team of A-players, and you work at it every day—the results after just one year will blow you away. You will have a group of people who understand your business, have the intelligence to learn quickly, and can take your business to the next level.

The messages of this book are simple, but powerful. You have to recruit the team that you need rather than just settle for the team that you have. You have to understand and follow the Three Steps for Building an A-Player Team: develop an A-player mind-set, interview all the time, and develop your company's "farm team." You have to recognize that building your company's brand attracts A-player employees as much as it attracts customers. Your managers and your employees have to work with you to find new A-players, and you must then develop good leadership practices to make your investment in these A-players pay off.

You can't be a great leader if you are not a great recruiter. Is there a college athletic coach whom you particularly admire? I guarantee you that his or her success on the field is directly tied to his or her recruiting prowess in the off-season. That person is an accomplished leader during games because he or she knows how to assemble the most talented individuals and lead them as a team.

It's no different in the professional world. The leaders who take a company from start-up through the small business stage to become industry leaders do so by assembling a great team of employees around them. This process can be challenging if the people who got your business to where it is today are incapable of taking it to the next level. In order to keep growing, you have to recruit the talent your business needs for *tomorrow*.

No matter your organization's current size, you need people who possess the hard and soft skills necessary to do a specific job. They must be proactive, willing to take ownership of their work, and able to think independently. They must be problem solvers. It often feels that such people are in depressingly short supply. This book is dedicated to helping you find them, hire them, and keep them. *How to Hire A-Players* is for you if:

- You and your inner-circle of employees can no longer run the business by yourselves.
- You recognize that the people who got you here are not sufficient to get you where you want to be. You need more A-players to achieve the next level of growth and profits.
- You are drowning in administrative and managerial duties and must hire strong people to free you up to do the things you do best.
- You have a good business but don't lead a balanced life. You want to enjoy your life while you build your business. You realize that you must surround yourself with a higher-quality team in order to accomplish both goals.
- Your business resembles a little kid's soccer team: everyone is scurrying after the ball, but no one is passing or playing his or her position. While this approach worked for a while, your

business now needs more skilled people who know how to get things done without your constant and intensive involvement.
- You have a vision for the A-player team you want. Now you want some proven, practical strategies for turning this vision into reality.

I focus this book on where and how to find A-players. I start by describing some key recruiting strategies and then ask you to determine the A-Player Profiles of key roles within your company. I end the book by discussing the importance of strong leadership for keeping the A-players that you hire. Sandwiched between these chapters is a wealth of real-life examples and explanations of where and how to find the A-players who will become your competitive advantage.

Let's get started!

1

The Value of A-Players

Almost no one wants to spend time on recruiting. You know it's important and has to get done, but you are busy. Typically, your team is shorthanded during the recruiting process. You have an open position, after all, which makes you even busier. So why take the time to read this book and commit to hiring A-player employees?

Thriving Businesses Are Built by Teams of A-Players

Nothing has a bigger impact on the results of your business and the quality of your life than hiring—and keeping—A-players. Perhaps you have a vision for growing your business, having a great life and career, and then selling your business one day for a sizable sum. If you don't hire great people, those dreams will fizzle. Dedicate yourself to hiring A-players today if you want to be a leader who turns this vision into a reality. Whether you have a sophisticated recruiting apparatus or not, you must figure out how to find, attract, and employ A-players. It is essential for success.

Chief executive officer of Meridian Enterprises Corporation Sam Toumayan started his company in 1978 as an incentive travel company. A number of Sam's peers founded similar companies around the same time. More than three decades later, Meridian stands as a transformative power in the sales incentive industry. Companies around the globe use its patented credit card–based programs. Meridian has changed this industry forever, while similar companies that started at the same time have gone out of business or been acquired.

What made the difference?

If you ask Sam, he will tell you that he hired strong people and trusted them to do their jobs well. Sam recognized that he had to recruit A-players and have them build the enterprise that he wanted. The difference between a business that fizzles and one that takes off is often whether the CEO knows how to hire and lead A-players.

> **A-Player Principle:** You have to be willing to let go of some control in order to grow your company. Do you currently have A-players on your team whom you can trust to lead some—or even *all*—of your business for you?

The Impact of Just One Great Hire

A-players have an exponential, not incremental, impact on your business. Microsoft has more than 80,000 employees worldwide. How much impact could one employee have on a business that size? Not much, right? Bill Gates believes otherwise. He claims that the entire company was really built around fewer than 20 people.[1] If Gates needed fewer than 20 people to become the wealthiest man in the world, what impact could just two or three *true* A-players have on *your* business—and your life?

I am convinced that most businesspeople are not committed to recruiting because they believe that hiring great people is a crapshoot. But hiring doesn't have to be a roll of the dice. While you can never eliminate all of the risk, there are certainly steps you can take that will result in bringing more A-players into your company. The question is: Will you and your company pledge to continually find and hire A-players? Is it worth the time and effort? The answer should be an enthusiastic YES—because adding just a few more A-players to your team can pay off in fantastic ways. Let's take a look at how much impact just one great hire can have on a business.

One A-Player Can Give You Your Life Back

Jody and Heather Herzog own a Fleet Feet Sports franchise in Cleveland, Ohio. This young, energetic couple ran a good business and had big plans for the future. They had a number of good employees, but as with many small businesses, the bulk of the responsibility for leading their specialty retail business fell on their shoulders. They served customers, bought product, oversaw the financials, ran training programs, created marketing campaigns, and dealt with the hundreds of other tasks that had to get done.

Then the Herzogs found Eddie, who happened to have 12 years of experience managing a competitor's store across town. He was bored with his current role and saw Fleet Feet as a great new career opportunity. Plus, he would likely have a shorter commute. Over a period of months, these factors were enough to get him to make the move and come to work for Heather and Jody. The impact was immediate. Eddie essentially started running the place. He used proven methods for improving buying and inventory. He brought specific ideas for new marketing programs. Eddie anticipated what needed to be done, and he did it.

Eddie began to mentor and lead the other staff. He set a positive pace and tone for other employees. In doing so, he helped to create a great company culture in which even average employees perform at their highest possible levels.

The impact of hiring one A-player was exponential, not incremental, for this business. After hiring Eddie, the Herzogs could focus their time on important activities for acquiring new customers, improving customer retention, and managing inventory levels to maximize profitability. In other words, the best people in the business got better because they had one more person on whom they could really depend. That process, repeated over and over, is how great businesses get built.

In addition to the business benefits, Eddie helped Jody and Heather to get their lives back. They don't have to spend every waking hour at their store. They can take a day off together and trust that the store will be run well in their absence. They gain some margin in their lives and again look forward to the days they spend in the store. Too many owners of small and midsize businesses have lives that are indistinguishable from their work. They have no time to themselves because without them, things fall apart. But one A-player like Eddie can change all of that. He or she can take responsibility for important pieces of the business, oversee other people, and even bring in new business. While no business can or should sit on the shoulders of one person, for Jody and Heather, this single key employee gives them the ability to keep building a great business without completely sacrificing their personal lives.

> **A-Player Principle:** Even one A-player can help you to build a great business—and have a full and satisfying life outside of work.

One A-Player Can Keep You from Getting Divorced

Whether literally or figuratively, you have to employ people to whom you trust "the keys" to your business. Executives and business owners who lack strong employees cannot take a vacation without worrying that their entire operation will be in ruins when they return. They cannot "turn the lights off" in the office of their mind or focus on the rest of their lives—which can result in train wrecks at home. Marriages become strained or even ruined when businesspeople don't have at least one A-player who can supervise in their absence. Hiring A-players and setting them up to succeed can help you to regain balance in your life—and keep your personal life as well as your business life on track.

I coach a number of business owners and senior managers who are A-players. They are personally effective and get a lot done. However, their strength becomes their weakness. Their employees don't take ownership and initiative because they know that "Jack or Lisa will do it." These clients of mine make every decision. If a new idea is going to be created, they create it. If a new program is going to be implemented, they implement it. Things can go on like this for only so long before the business and their personal lives suffer. One of the best things you can do for the long-term success of your career and your life is to hire people who can move the ball forward in your business without you.

> **A-Player Principle:** Finding and hiring A-players may save your marriage and key personal relationships.

One A-Player Can Help You to Sell Your Business

Do you have an exit plan from your business? Is your retirement plan contingent on being able to sell your company for a meaningful sum? Have you had your business valued? How much money is at stake for you personally if it is estimated to be less than you think it is worth?

Business valuation expert Vic Haas says that "when buyers look at your business, they must be convinced that [it] can survive without you." When Vic is hired to value a private business for sale, one factor he always examines is the compensation of top executives. He wants to know if there is anyone in the business who is worth a big salary other than the owner. Having a management team comprised of a bunch of poorly compensated average performers reduces the company's value. Vic wants to see a corporation in which future growth and daily operations are driven by people other than the owner. Potential buyers for your business know this. They will assess the quality of your team as part of their own due diligence.

When viewed in this light, you can see how hiring A-players has a direct impact on the value of your business and your net worth. Most businesspeople understand that they need to create systems and processes that operate without their involvement. But you have

> **A-Player Principle:** Selling your business for the price you want may depend on having A-players who can run it for you. Would a potential buyer today believe that you have an A-player management team?

to have people who can run these systems effectively. If you hope to sell your business one day, you should be hiring A-players right now to build and run it.

You Can't Turn Midgets into Giants

How well do your current employees respond to coaching and training? Do they produce great results after you invest time in them? If your answer to these questions is "not well," you have to examine both the effectiveness of your leadership and the talent of your people.

Coaching and developing your staff is vital for improving performance and retaining good employees. I have helped numerous executives, managers, and key employees increase their business value in this respect. But don't fool yourself into thinking that you can turn a C-player into an A-player. You can't turn midgets into giants. Look around your organization. If you see one person whose performance is head and shoulders above everyone else, chances are that she was already a superior performer (or at least had superior talents) when you hired her. Get committed to finding more of these people. The best way to make your investment in your staff pay off is to coach A-players!

> **A-Player Principle:** Don't try to solve a recruiting problem with a coaching solution. You can't turn midgets into giants.

The Best Coaches Are the Best Recruiters

I am a devoted fan of the St. Louis Cardinals. Pitching coach Dave Duncan is legendary for taking pitchers, who used to win 15 games per year but now only win 7 or 8, and getting them back to the top of their game. He is so good that there is talk of making him the first pitching coach to be added to the Major League Baseball Hall of Fame.

Do you think that if a pitcher with great ability has been on a losing streak and then gets the chance to play for Dave Duncan, he would do everything in his power to make it happen? You better believe he would. By playing for Duncan and the Cardinals, such a pitcher could add years to his career and millions to his bank account.

The dynamics (if not the salary levels) are the same in every industry and business. The best coaches are the best recruiters. They excel at selling their program to A-players. A-players want to keep improving; that is part of what makes them so good. You recruit A-players in part by showing them that you can help them to reach the next level in their career.

Progressive Business Publications provides newsletters, books, and online training via a sales force of 550 telemarketers in 15 locations across the United States. The vice president of sales, Colin Drummond, is the Dave Duncan of Progressive. He places a huge emphasis on instructing and developing salespeople. He requires his team leaders to be coaches, not just managers. They spend their time asking questions so that salespeople are forced to think for themselves, diagnose their own problems, and take ownership of the solutions. His telemarketers are typically making $9 to $12 an hour. Yet as Colin says, "People will take $1.50 less per hour at Progressive because they know that they're being developed." The strong sales coaching at Progressive—and the leadership's commitment to helping salespeople achieve—is a competitive advantage that allows the company to attract and keep people in a very cost-effective manner.

A-Player Principle: Recruit A-players by showing them how you can help them to reach the next level in their career.

Get Passionate about Finding and Hiring A-Players

As Barney Kister, senior vice president of sales and operations for Supplies Network, says, "You should never hire just to fill a position. You should always be looking for good people to add to your team." If you start to think about recruiting only *after* a position has opened up, you have already lost. Don't just fill empty roles. Define the team you need to achieve your goals. Then work constantly to put that team in place.

Make Money Next Year from the A-Players You Hire This Year

Legendary sales trainer Bill Brooks once worked for a billionaire who owned multiple companies across the country. He asked this man what the secret to building a great business was. "Make money next year from things you sell this year" was one of the billionaire's replies.

If you think about it, this principle applies directly to finding and hiring A-players. The investment of time that you make in finding great employees this year will pay off for you for years to come. Hiring A-players is one of the best investments you can make, and the only way to do this consistently is to implement a good recruiting system. Develop a passion for recruiting and pass that passion along to your executives and managers. Communicate the importance of building a great team and respect the time that they spend networking and recruiting. Create a culture where people strategize about finding A-players.

Focus on the Value of A-Players

Focus on the value of hiring just one more A-player instead of worrying about the time it will take to do so. As British physicist Lord Kelvin said, "When you can measure what you are speaking about, and express it in numbers, you know something about it; but when you cannot measure it, when you cannot express it in numbers, your knowledge of it is of a meager and unsatisfactory kind."[2]

Executives shy away from recruiting processes because they have a clear sense of their costs—the time and effort that takes them away from their "real jobs"—but not of the benefits. They are not completely convinced that their own recruiting and interviewing efforts will pay off in more A-player employees.

The programs described in this book don't cost a lot of money to implement. But they do require time and commitment. You have to sell yourself and your team on the importance of recruiting. Put some numbers to the impact that better talent will have on your organization. If you start paying more attention to the quality of people you hire and follow the steps I outline in the following chapters, the overall talent level in your organization will rise. You will hire people who produce better results and increase your team's productivity. Hiring just a handful of A-players in the near future will have a powerful impact on your business. You don't have to find 100 extraordinarily high-caliber people to create a measurable improvement in results; just one great hire could make all the difference for you.

Simply buying this book has demonstrated your willingness to do what it takes to build a superior team. Investment always precedes return. The steps you are taking today will result in a team that can fulfill your vision tomorrow.

A-Players Beget A-Players

Talent begets talent. Merely hiring one A-player begins to create an environment where other A-players *want* to work. Conversely, if you don't devote time and energy to hiring more A-players, the ones you already have may leave. Carl Gersbach, managing director of Brokerage Services in Philadelphia for CB Richard Ellis, put it this way: "The minute you bring the wrong person into the group, you create a situation where strong people who have always said that they would never leave now might consider it, because the environment within the organization has changed."

Carl strongly emphasizes the importance of recruiting and hiring. Not only does he understand the value of A-players, he knows the risks and costs of hiring weaker players. Over the long haul, it is not enough to have just one A-player employee who is surrounded by weaker team members. Most A-players have a strong desire to learn, grow, and develop. One of the ways they do this is by working with other great people. If your team is one Great Dane surrounded by Chihuahuas, your "big dog" is at risk. One of your competitors simply needs to convince that person that he or she will have greater professional development opportunities with them rather than with you.

> **A-Player Principle:** If you don't keep hiring A-players, the ones you already have may start leaving.

Isn't This HR's Job?

You may be wondering, "But isn't this HR's job?" If you have a strong human resources and/or recruiting department, it *can* be a tremendous asset in finding and recruiting A-players. But as a leader in the business, you must own ultimate responsibility for improving the talent in your company. Hiring A-players is a business priority, not just an HR priority.

In addition, the ability to hire A-players rises and falls on relationships. A great recruiter provides you with leverage in reaching A-players. However, you and your managers also have professional relationships and networks. You are the ones who are—or should be—rubbing shoulders with the best and brightest in your field. While HR can do a lot of the groundwork, it ultimately cannot make an A-player come to work for you. It is *your* responsibility to discern which individuals could make a major contribution to your team.

Hiring A-players is an ongoing commitment to creating a team that achieves superior results, so don't get lazy if you find one great person. Instead, use that person as the foundation for an A-player team. While your HR contact or recruiter can be a great resource for reaching out to these people, *you* have to drive the process.

The 80/20 Principle Is Alive and Well

If you want to convince yourself of the impact which A-players will have on your business and your life, step back and assess your current team. How much more productive are the top 20 percent versus the other 80 percent?

AirClic is a Pennsylvania-based company that sells solutions for automating mobile work processes by using cell phones to capture and track data. Its customers include airlines, manufacturers, health-care companies, and others. But the company faced a challenge: Many prospective customers were excited about the solution, but this highly technical sale required buy-in from both financial and technical decision makers within these corporations. While salespeople could open the doors, they needed help to persuade prospective clients of the technical merits of the system.

To accomplish this, CEO Tim Bradley and his executives retooled their internal consulting group to provide technical sales support and they used their A-players to do it. While every consultant on the team had strong technical skills, a handful of them also had especially keen communication skills and personal presence. These people could explain the company's solutions in terms that both technical and nontechnical buyers could understand. AirClic took this handful of persuasive technical consultants and teamed them up with their salespeople.

Now, when AirClic salespeople line up a meeting with a prospective client, they take their A-player technical consultants along with them. The consultants bring technical credibility to the sales process, but they also know how to move the sale forward rather than getting bogged down in technical minutiae. The results? AirClic's sales have increased significantly due to the company's ability to identify a talent choke point and deploy A-players to solve it. AirClic recognized that 20 percent of its internal consultants were A-players who could help to drive sales as well as implement solutions. By focusing on this 20 percent and actively recruiting more people like them, the company was able to move its sales results to the next level.

Where Are Your Talent Choke Points?

Now bring this type of evaluation to your own company. Where are the talent "choke points" in your business? What results will be attainable only if you employ higher-caliber people? What positions in your organization are capable of turbo-charging your sales and profitability if they are filled with A-players? Examples include:

- **Sales.** Salespeople who can find new prospects, marshal internal resources well, and manage accounts after the sale.
- **Sales management.** Sales managers who know your industry, can earn the trust of your sales force, and serve as leaders and coaches.
- **Marketing.** Marketing managers who can design campaigns that more effectively drive leads for your sales organization. They go beyond tactics. They understand how marketing drives new customer acquisition.
- **Project management.** Project managers who ensure that an internal team hits its deadlines and interact well with clients. They free up others in your firm to spend more time on business development and less time managing existing accounts.
- **Store management.** Store managers who are leaders, not just doers. They improve sales and customer satisfaction by knowing how to put a great store team in place.
- **Financial leadership.** Financial executives and managers who get the financial reporting and monthly close processes under control and help the rest of the company make better business decisions by being strong strategists and internal advisors.

This list can go on and on, but you get the point. Every company has roles in which A-players produce quantifiably better financial results than do B- and C-players. Find those roles, define the A-player profile for that role, and lead your team through the processes I describe in this book to find your A-players. The impact to your top and bottom line will be powerful.

> **A-Player Principle:** Every business has talent choke points. There is no excuse for not recruiting A-players for these roles.

Challenge Your Leadership Team

If you buy into what I am saying, then challenge your leadership team to focus on finding and hiring A-players. Do not assume that they are already committed to this goal. Though it's impossible to argue with the statement "We have to hire better people," you want more than an absence of argument. Why will hiring more A-players in particular roles pay off in your company? Get your leaders involved in a conversation about the potential benefits of committing to an A-player hiring strategy. The very act of articulating the benefits will help them buy into the plan.

Payoffs from This Management Discussion

You accomplish four things by having this conversation with your leaders.

1. You stress the fact that hiring and keeping talent is a priority for you, not just a topic to which you pay lip service. Hiring A-players is a goal that you will both emphasize and measure.
2. You make sure that your department heads and team leaders are thinking objectively about the talent on their teams. Many managers lose perspective regarding their people. They identify with their own team more than they do with the company and *its* leadership team. Your job is to bring them back to a more accurate perspective on where and how to make their teams stronger.

3. You determine whether your current leaders know A-players in and out of your industry. The best business leaders are networked and aware of the level of talent that is available out there. They know how their people measure up against this benchmark.

4. You assess the quality of your own leadership team. Do your leaders perceive a need for better talent on their teams? Furthermore, would *you* want to work for them? Why or why not? And if you wouldn't want to work for them, what makes you think that other A-players would?

> **A-Player Principle:** Involvement creates buy-in, so involve your leaders in a conversation about an A-player hiring strategy. The very act of articulating the benefits will help them own and execute a plan.

The Team You Need versus the Team You Have

In the movie *Searching for Bobby Fischer*, about the development of a chess prodigy, a young chess player sits across a chess board from his coach, who is trying to teach him to plan his moves four, five, or six steps ahead. The young boy struggles to do so—all he sees before him is a board crowded with pieces. Finally, in frustration, the coach swipes his arm across the board and knocks all the pieces to the ground. "Now do you see it?" he asks the boy. "Don't focus on the pieces; you have to see the whole board."

Building an organization is like that. You can get so caught up in the separate "pieces" that comprise your current team that you fail to see the "whole board"—the team you *need* to achieve your goals. In his best-selling book *The E-Myth Revisited*, author Michael Gerber points out that creating an organizational chart can force you to define what you need accomplished apart from the people you currently employ.[3] Review or create your own organizational chart, and define excellence and key results for each role. Then write the names of the people you employ into the roles you've defined. As you complete this exercise, it is likely that gaps will begin to emerge between the job that needs to be done and the people you currently have. While many of us tolerate poor performance in key roles, we need to have the courage to admit that one or more of our team members are not doing—and will not be able to do—the jobs that need to be done. By acknowledging this, we do our companies, our teams, and ourselves a great favor.

Believe it or not, the strategies in this book will not only help you to find better people, they will help you to confront poor performance more effectively. Often executives and managers don't deal with inadequate workers because they don't have anyone to take their places. The strategies in this book give you a pipeline of talent to help solve both problems. Interested? Then read on.

A-Player Payoff Points

Chapter 1: The Value of A-Players

- If you want to build a substantial business, you must stop being a control freak. Start hiring A-players, and let them build your business for you.
- Hiring A-players is critical to building the company you want while having a life with which you are happy.
- Potential buyers for your business will check to see if you employ A-players who can run the business without you. If you don't, the value of your business goes down.
- Stop trying to turn C-players into A-players. It doesn't work.
- The best coaches are the best recruiters. They attract great talent, incorporate it into their system, and produce winning teams.

(continued)

(*continued*)

- Recruiting A-players is everyone's job, not just the job of human resources.
- Stop hiring to fill positions. Start making every hire a piece of the puzzle in building a great team.
- Recruiting is not a necessary evil. Start viewing recruiting as a competitive advantage.
- It is likely that the team you have is not the team you need to get your business where you want it to be. Get committed to finding the right players for your team.

2 Would You Know an A-Player if You Met One?

Defining Your A-Player Profile

I have a terrific client who owns an award-winning kitchen and bath design firm. When Bill and I started working together, he had recently created the position of showroom sales manager—and promptly hired then fired three people for the role. What was the problem?

When Bill hired these people, he was looking for a "hunter" who would prospect for new business. We created an A-Player Profile for the position and realized that this skill was much less important than the ability to close sales and manage kitchen remodeling jobs. None of the three employees who were hired (and subsequently fired) had any project management skills or experience. They could prospect for new business, but they couldn't complete quality projects. As a result, they did a poor job for their clients and failed to generate strong referrals. While they had sales skills, they did not have the right skills for *this* sales position. In other words, Bill had intentionally hired people who could not do the job!

You can't consistently hit a goal if you don't see it clearly. Bill is an example of a successful person who fell into a common trap. He couldn't hire great people because he had not taken the time to define what it meant to do the job very well. He needed to identify an A-Player Profile for the key roles in his company. For this showroom sales manager position, the A-Player Profile was someone who could convert walk-in prospects into clients *and* manage the details of product pricing and project management. Once Bill defined this profile, his hiring results improved by leaps and bounds. He stopped losing time, wasting money, and squandering opportunities because of sub-par hiring decisions. Knowing exactly whom he needed in the role helped him to avoid making the same mistakes over and over. The same can be true for you and your business.

> **A-Player Principle:** Companies "intentionally" hire the wrong people all the time. If you're not clear on what makes someone an A-player in a role, you are destined to make very expensive hiring mistakes.

Where Do I Start?

Sometimes it makes sense to pay top dollar for a new employee. In other situations, however, you want to be a "value investor" by recruiting and hiring talented people who are underrated in the market. Either way, you have to know *who* you are looking for by developing a clear picture of your A-Player Profile. Then you are ready to out-recruit your competition. At the end of this chapter, I will lead you through the process of determining an A-Player Profile. First, let's look at some success stories.

Case Study: Inside Sales and the Most Assertive Customer Service People

Supplies Network wholesales business machine and computer supplies (data storage media, laser cartridges, etc.) to dealers nationwide. By determining its A-Player Profile for sales, the company has consistently and successfully targeted and recruited the right individuals and built an industry-leading team. Its inside sales reps are responsible for making outbound client calls, developing customer relationships, taking incoming orders, and ensuring that customers' orders are delivered complete and on time.

The company hired people with a range of different backgrounds for the inside sales role. The job requires a lot of the same skills and experiences that customer service representatives gain working in a call center. But this is a true sales position; reps have to be able to prospect, open relationships, and ask for business. The Supplies Network management team looked carefully at those individuals who did well as sales reps and those who did not. Many with typical outside sales profiles floundered because they lacked detail orientation and follow-up skills. Others were very customer-service focused but couldn't open new accounts or proactively seek more business from existing customers.

As a result, the A-Player Profile for inside sales at Supplies Network is an assertive, people-oriented individual who can prospect and also deliver consistent customer service. Early in the company's growth, this led to an innovative advertising strategy. Supplies Network ran ads for customer service representatives despite the fact that it was filling sales positions. Knowing its A-Player Profile enabled the organization to expand its pool of candidates from people with proven inside sales experience to anyone with customer service experience. Next, it used assessment tools to identify the most assertive and outgoing of these candidates. This cut the pool down to customer service people with a sales profile. Finally, company managers interviewed the candidates to assess their sales skills and customer orientation.

A-Player Principle: Find a large pool of people who have the basic skills you are looking for, interview a lot of them, and hire the best. That is a simple formula for consistently hiring A-players.

Supplies Network used classified advertising successfully early on, and it has grown from revenue of $70 million in 1999 to approximately $400 million today. To find the right people to support and fuel this progress, the company's recruiting strategies have developed as well. Today, the company relies more on referrals and less on advertising, but it still knows exactly what kind of person it's looking to hire. Senior Vice President of Sales and Operations Barney Kister, introduced in Chapter 1, starts from the premise that although there are a lot of good people out there, you have to work to find them. He tells us, "If you want an organization of top-notch people, you have to invest time in building it. It's just like getting into top physical shape. You don't work out one day per week; you create a habit of working out three, four, or five days per week. Building a team of great people is the same way." If you have a vision of the A-player team that you want, you have to work every day to create it.

As a result of this commitment, Supplies Network interviews a lot of potential salespeople—whether there happens to be a position currently open or not. In Barney's words, "We interview people all the time. We never try to hire just to fill a position. We are continually looking for good people to add to our team. Like everyone else, we have attrition, and we always want to know people who can fill those holes."

Barney also understands that most of the people he interviews are not A-players. When he does uncover a superior salesperson, he hires him or her on the spot. "When I find great people, I hire them whether or not I have an opening. I often tell people when I hire them, 'I have no idea what you will end up doing for us, but we will work it out in the next month or so.'"

Case Study: Who Makes the Best Accounting Firm Partner?

A large accounting firm used to emphasize hiring graduates from Ivy League schools. Many of the firm's partners were graduates of these schools, and graduates from these institutions certainly had the brainpower to do the tax and audit job well. However, the firm found after it hired these young employees that it struggled to keep them around long enough to make them partners. The problem was significant enough that the firm began to analyze its employee base and to determine its own A-Player Profile.

The firm found that while most of the Ivy League graduates recruited right out of college left after a few years (as it had suspected), many graduates of the "next-tier" schools often stayed with the firm and became partners. It turned out that the Ivy League grads had many friends and schoolmates employed on Wall Street who were making a lot more money than they were.

Would You Know an A-Player if You Met One? **25**

The lower compensation and relative lack of prestige was enough to persuade them to leave for other jobs or for graduate school after only a few years of employment. However, graduates of the next-tier schools did not feel this same pressure. In their and their peers' opinions, becoming a partner at this firm was highly prestigious, and the money was excellent compared to what most of their contemporaries were making.

This firm was smart and flexible enough to switch its recruiting efforts. The results were powerful and long-lasting. It started hiring aggressively out of these second-tier schools and saw a big jump in retention of A-players. Knowing its A-Player Profile made the difference between hiring recent college grads who left in three years versus hiring those who stayed with the firm, became partners, and generated millions of dollars of fees over the course of their careers.

> **A-Player Principle:** Just because people went to the "right" schools or worked for big companies in your industry does not make them A-players. Don't follow the herd when it comes to recruiting. Instead, define the profile that works in your unique environment.

Case Study: The Single-Mother Waitress

Doorway Rug in Buffalo, New York, makes a very good business out of cleaning the mats that lie at the doors of almost every commercial building. (The company was recently acquired by Cintas, the major player in this business.) Salespeople go door-to-door to businesses selling this service. When Doorway Rug looked at its best salespeople, it recognized one common

(continued)

(*continued*)

profile: many of them were single mothers who had been wait-resses. Though this may sound like a strange A-Player Profile, when you consider the following points, it makes perfect sense.

- The best waitresses (and waiters) are salespeople, not just order takers. They are always providing their customers with options and "up-selling."
- They are excellent multitaskers; after all, that's how they keep seven tables of customers happy at one time.
- The hours in the restaurant industry are terrible, particularly if you have a family.

In this light, everyone should be hiring the best people out of Applebee's and Chili's. In fact, Doorway Rug found that it could hire former waitresses to be salespeople and pay them roughly the same amount they were making at restaurants. The reduced and flexible hours that Doorway Rug offered attracted women who supported children and families on their own. These candidates valued the opportunity to make a good living and be at home in the afternoon to greet the school bus.

As Paul Van De Putte, former chief executive and president of Doorway Rug, explains: "Hiring single-mother waitresses to be salespeople was a repeatable recruiting formula for us. Your typical Applebee's waitress is outgoing, good with people, and willing to do hard work. We gave them a step up in prestige at about the same money they were making at the restaurant, but they didn't have to work nights or weekends with us. We were flexible in terms of giving them time to get their kids off the bus and handle their other responsibilities at home."

Doorway Rug leveraged its A-Player Profile to recruit in ways its competitors did not. One of its strategies was running employment ads focused specifically on restaurant personnel. As Paul describes: "To find people, we ran ads in the restaurant sections of the classifieds under the waiter/waitress heading. We interviewed them, hired the best, and trained them in our sales system."

> **A-Player Principle:** Knowing your A-Player Profile helps you to attract candidates whom your competitors are overlooking.

Interview More People!

Companies like Supplies Network and Doorway Rug know their A-Player Profile and use it to cast a wide recruiting net. Then they cull through countless job applicants to find the A-players. In contrast, companies that lack an A-Player Profile don't focus their recruiting efforts and often don't interview enough candidates. I get calls all the time from companies that want me to assess two finalists for an open position. The conversation goes like this:

Eric: "So Janet, you have narrowed it down to two candidates for this position?"

Janet: "Yes."

Eric: "How many candidates did you interview in total for this position?"

Janet: "Two."

Eric: "Janet, without looking at any testing results for these candidates, I can already give you my recommendation. Between Candidate One and Candidate Two, I really like Candidate Three."

If you want to hire better employees, you must *interview more people*. Supplies Network, for example, did a great job of expanding its candidate pool by advertising for customer service people when in fact it was hiring salespeople. The company knew how to separate true salespeople from order takers in the interview process. It also interviewed job candidates constantly, even if it did not have a position to fill. Taken together, these tactics allowed Supplies Network to avoid the classic mistake of interviewing only one or two people for a job and then wondering why a new hire is mediocre.

If a salesperson talked to only one or two prospects, he would not be surprised that his sales results were terrible. As a recruiter, the same principle applies. You must talk to more qualified people.

> **A-Player Principle:** Hiring is a numbers game. The more qualified people you talk to, the better your chances of making a great hire. Tap into a large pool of qualified candidates, weed out most of them, and then select the best of those left standing.

Get Better Results from Job Advertisements

Like Supplies Network, Doorway Rug used its A-Player Profile to increase the effectiveness of its job postings. Instead of advertising for the position in the sales section, it advertised in the restaurant section. This unlikely approach worked; many of its best salespeople applied for the position when they had intended to continue waiting on tables. Once the company knew its A-Player Profile, this was the only logical way to publicize it.

The ability to define an A-Player Profile can turbo-charge the results of your "help wanted" advertising, whether in traditional or online media. Yes, some unqualified applicants will apply. Deal with it. Salespeople do not protest if a lot of prospects seek them out, even if it means more time spent qualifying. Recruiting is just marketing and sales in different clothes. It's simple: the more prospective job candidates you have, the more great hires you will make.

How to Define Your A-Player Profile

An A-Player Profile specifies the combination of skills and experience that will make someone a probable A-player in your business. Once you know what this is, you are ready to move into recruiting mode. Ten steps you can take to determine your A-Player Profile are presented next. Take the time to write down your answers.

1. Pick a key position in your organization.
2. Define success for this position in two to three sentences. In other words, what happens when someone performs well in the role?
3. Break this overall picture of success into specific key results: five to seven specific, observable indicators to let you know someone is performing well in this role. Gather input from other people who understand the job. You may find that you want results out of the position that no one has been able to produce to date, which is fine. Part of defining your A-Player Profile often involves refocusing the job itself.
4. Now, write down the names of *all* the people who are or have been in the position (not just the A-players). How do the most successful employees go about creating the key results you just described? What steps do they take? What actions do they avoid? In contrast, what do your B and C-players do (or fail to do) that causes their performance to lag behind that of the A-players?
5. Take your best shot at writing down the skills, talents, and experiences required to create superior results.
6. Next, ask yourself this question: are the A-players superior because of skills that can be *learned* easily or because of talents that are difficult—if not impossible—to teach? To the extent that A-players are good because of their natural skills and abilities, you have to recruit people who already have these skills. This is a critical piece of your A-Player Profile and an essential insight that will focus your recruiting efforts.
7. What are the employment and educational backgrounds of the A-players? Where and how did they develop the abilities that you value so highly? How do their backgrounds compare with that of the B and C-players?
8. How did each of these employees come to work for you? Where were they working previously?
9. Based on all this evaluation, where are some likely sources of candidates that you can tap into?
10. How can you promote the job to these people and begin creating a flow of candidates?

> **A-Player Principle:** When you discern the talents and abilities that distinguish A-players from other employees, you can focus your recruiting efforts. Often you start concentrating on candidates you previously overlooked.

Documenting Your A-Player Profile

By answering the questions in the last section, you give yourself enough information to develop a picture of what separates the best employees from everyone else. In visual form, define it as shown in Figure 2.1.

At the base of the pyramid for any position are the fundamental job requirements: the things you must do relatively well or get fired.

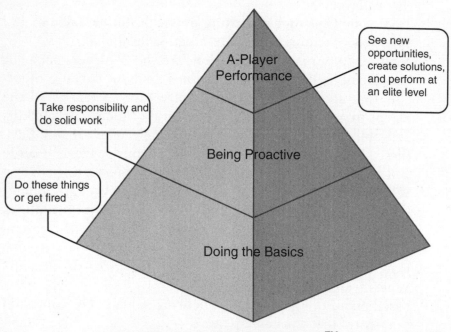

FIGURE 2.1 Performance Pyramid™

In the middle of the pyramid are the results that reasonably talented people can accomplish. At the top of the pyramid are the key results that A-players are able to produce. The value created by A-players often towers over everything else listed.

Here is an example of how these three levels of key results might look for a retail store inventory manager:

Doing the Basics

- Product is received at the shipping dock.
- Product is entered into the inventory system upon receipt.
- Physical inventory is stored in the correct places.
- Shipping and receiving area is clean and orderly.

Being Proactive
In addition to the basics just listed:

- Active communication with the product buyers ensures that the company always has appropriate levels of inventory.

A-Player Performance
In addition to all the above:

- Leverage the company's existing computer systems to further automate the inventory management process.
- Give sales staff confidence that inventory levels are accurate and products are available to be sold.
- Create more efficient inventory turns.

A-Player Principle: It is easy to do a job reasonably well. What does it look like to do it extraordinarily well? That's the start of your A-Player Profile.

Using Your A-Player Profile to Improve Recruiting Results

Once you have defined your A-Player Profile, use it to identify pools of individuals who have the foundational skills needed for the job. Reach out to these people. A well-defined A-Player Profile often allows a business to expand its recruiting net beyond people with industry experience. For instance, I know of a company in the marketing services business that insisted on hiring people with industry experience—despite the fact that its top two salespeople had none. This company's A-players sold beer and printing respectively prior to working for this company.

Companies often believe that they must hire people with industry experience because they cannot afford to invest the time to get a "newbie" up to speed. But hiring people with industry experience often means hiring the people your competitor just fired. You would think that if a company had successfully employed top performers from outside the industry, it would focus its ongoing recruiting efforts outside the industry. But frequently this is not the case. Companies tend to prefer the safety of hiring knowledgeable mediocrity to finding great potential wherever it may be currently employed. Defining your A-Player Profile is the first step to recruiting people with the right talent—no matter what their experience.

> **A-Player Principle:** The best companies often hire people without industry experience so they can train them right the first time. Though industry experience can be important, qualities like talent and drive are always more valuable than the number of years someone worked for your competitor.

Get Clear on Your "Knockout Factors"

Knowing your A-Player Profile also helps you to define "knockout factors"—those skills and abilities that a job candidate must possess or be "knocked out" of contention for the job. Supplies Network, for instance, knows the profile of its salespeople: assertive, people-oriented, impatient, and somewhat nonconformist. Even with sales and/or customer service background, you are knocked out of contention for the job if you lack this profile.

The interview process is a negative one for an employer because its primary purpose is to *eliminate* candidates who cannot or will not do the job. The problem I have seen many companies run into is that, because they have not defined their A-Player Profile, their knockout factors are either far too restrictive or simply don't exist. If your knockout factors are too restrictive, then *no* candidate will be good enough for you. But if you don't have any knockout factors, your interview and hiring process is uninformed. You try to hire all kinds of people to do a job and make great hires only by sheer luck.

A-Player Principle: When you define your knockout factors, you know how to eliminate people from the interview process. People who lack these key skills are immediately out of contention; the people left standing get a second look.

Case Study: Knowing Your Knockout Factors

Maryann Vitale can explain her knockout factors to you in detail, which is one of the reasons she is such an effective recruiter. Maryann is a successful broker/owner for Prudential Real Estate, and her primary job is recruiting new agents. While she does hire some agents with real estate experience, she also looks for many brand-new prospects who have never

(continued)

(*continued*)

sold a piece of real estate in their lives. These agents come from all different walks of life; they are stay-at-home moms, businesspeople, and recent college graduates. Maryann has two primary criteria for identifying her A-players, whatever their background:

- Do they know a lot of people?
- Are they deal *makers* rather than just deal takers?

For Maryann, someone is a deal maker if he or she naturally thinks about how to overcome obstacles in order to make a deal happen. In her interview process, she often gives candidates this scenario:

"You, the job candidate, are the seller's agent for a home. The buyer and his agent have told you and your client that they will buy your house "as is," without any contingencies. The house inspection is completed, and you are close to having a deal. Then the buyer's agent comes back to you and asks for $5,000 of concessions to deal with issues uncovered during the inspection. In other words, the buyer and his agent have gone back on their promise. What do you do?"

Maryann says that people respond to this scenario in two distinct ways. The first group says, "Can they really do that? That doesn't seem fair." The second group says, "Well, let's see . . . there has to be a way to make the deal work."

The "deal makers" fit Maryann's A-Player Profile. They will actively work to keep a deal alive rather than just accept that a transaction is unraveling. The "deal takers"—those left speechless by Maryann's hypothetical real estate transaction—are out. They don't have what it takes to be an A-player in Maryann's business.

A-Player Principle: When you interview, ask questions that test prospective employees against your knockout factors. This saves you time and helps you to focus your recruiting efforts on potential A-players.

A-Player Payoff Points

Chapter 2: Would You Know an A-Player if You Met One? Defining Your A-Player Profile

- Companies "intentionally" hire the wrong people all the time, so define your A-Player Profile early on to avoid shooting yourself in the foot.
- Know the skills that people must bring with them to the job versus the skills that you can teach them. Defining your A-Player Profile allows you to hone in on what makes people A-players in the first place.
- Your A-Player Profile helps you to identify the right places to look for would-be hires. It often leads you to pools of candidates that your competitors are overlooking.
- In the end, hiring is a numbers game. You have to interview a lot of qualified people to find an A-player. Your A-Player Profile allows you to cast a wide net, run a lot of people through your interview system, and hire the true standouts.
- Just because people went to a prestigious school or worked for one of your biggest competitors does not mean they are A-players. You have to dig in to understand the profile of the person who excels in your environment.
- Whether your A-Player Profile is a "single-mother waitress" or something completely different, understanding what motivates your top performers helps you to attract A-players to come to work for you.

(continued)

(continued)

- When you define your knockout factors, you know how to eliminate people from consideration quickly. This helps you to avoid hiring mistakes and lets you focus your time and energy on hiring the A-players.

3

Three Steps to Creating an A-Player Team

N ow that you know what an A-player looks like for key roles in your company, how do you start finding better talent? Here are three steps to take to create an A-player team.

First of all, you and your company have to adopt an A-player mind-set by demonstrating that you are constantly on the lookout for the best people. While most executives talk a good game here, in reality, their recruiting efforts are sporadic at best. Your focus on finding A-players must be ongoing and consistent.

Second, you and your leadership team must interview *all the time*. You have to develop a reputation as an organization that is always interested in meeting good people and willing to talk with them. This is the only way to develop a strong pipeline of potential employees from which to select A-players.

Third, you have to build a "farm team" of talented people who work for someone else right now but would be thrilled to work for you in the future. The key here is to have a continually updated list of A-players who could fit right into your company and make a big contribution. If you and your leadership team are regularly cultivating your farm team, you will always have strong people to turn to when you want to hire someone.

A-Player Principle: There are three steps to building an A-player team:

1. Create an A-player mind-set throughout your company.
2. Interview all the time.
3. Develop a farm team.

Create an A-Player Mind-Set

Chris Burkhard is president of CBI Group, a project/on-demand recruitment firm in Newark, Delaware. Chris found himself in the uncomfortable position of having to lay off employees because of a difficult economy. After years of double-digit growth and accolades from the business community, this was an especially painful experience. One day, after CBI Group had just laid off several people, another employee told him about a friend of his who was looking for a job. "I know you tell us that we're always looking for good people, but I'm sure it's not appropriate for us to interview anyone right now," the employee said. Chris looked at the friend's resume, thought for a moment, and said, "I was always taught that you 'keep your couch full' of potential employees. We have to always know where our next hire is coming from. Let's interview your friend."

Had Chris created a company-wide mind-set that you always, always look for A-player talent? Clearly, he had; otherwise, this employee would never have mentioned his friend's resume. Did Chris really *want* to interview prospective employees immediately following a layoff? No. But he did it anyway, because he understood that finding A-players is a discipline to which companies must be committed in both good times and bad. If this interviewee turned out to be a dead hit for one of the company's A-Player Profiles, at least he would be a valuable addition to the company's farm team.

Everyone with whom you and your colleagues come in contact must know that you are *always* interested in meeting talented people. You want your company's name to flash in the minds of your employees, customers, vendors—and everyone else you know—when they come across a great person looking to make a career move. To accomplish this, you must develop a reputation as the company to which people always refer top talent.

Creating an A-player mind-set motivates everyone in your network to scout for quality employees for your company. So few organizations deliver on this commitment to find and hire A-players that when you actually do so, your entire network starts paying attention and providing help. All of Chris Burkhard's associates knew that CBI Group was committed to looking for talent because Chris repeated this message and modeled the corresponding behavior. He and his senior managers were always interviewing people and rewarding those who provided the referrals. Chris's mantra was

"Always keep your couch full," something he reiterated so frequently that his team made fun of him for saying it so much. That's when he knew that his message was getting through.

A-Player Principle: When everyone inside and outside your organization knows that you're always interested in interviewing talented people, you have succeeded in creating an A-player mind-set.

Interview All the Time

The second step to creating an A-player team is to interview *all the time*. If you claim to have an A-player mind-set, you have to deliver on this by continually (not periodically) interviewing people. Every business with which I work that has superior recruiting results has a consistent flow of job candidates through its offices. This does not mean that you should (or could) interview people every single day. It works well in most organizations for each member of a leadership team to commit to interviewing two people per month. If there are seven people on your management team and you each interview two people per month, you will have met with 168 potential employees in a year. Chances are you will find a few A-players in the process!

Interviewing regularly makes the A-player mind-set work. If, for example, you want to get into top physical shape but only exercise intermittently and don't make any changes to your diet, how will your results be? Probably pretty lousy. To do things well, we must do them consistently. Your vision for building a great team has to show up in your weekly calendar. At some level, recruiting and hiring is a numbers game: If you interview more people, you will find more A-players. Every idea in this book is focused on filling your talent pipeline with a higher number of quality candidates. The way to take advantage of these expanded pools of talent is to make interviewing a regular part of your business schedule rather than a periodic necessary evil in which you reluctantly participate.

There is a saying in sales: customers buy when they are ready to buy something, not when we are ready to sell something. The same principle holds true in recruiting. People change employers—and even careers—for *their* reasons, not ours. A fixed schedule of interviewing allows you to initiate relationships with people now who will come to work for you down the road. This is the kind of strategic approach to recruiting that most business owners and executives believe they are too busy to execute. If you are the exception, it will pay off in more A-players who will take your business to a new level of success.

> **A-Player Principle:** Have each member of your leadership team interview at least two to three new people per month. The time commitment is reasonable, and the payoff from having a pipeline of talent for your company is significant.

But What if I Don't Have a Job to Fill?

When I tell executives that they should be interviewing all the time, they often tell me that they can't—because they don't have a position to fill. What they don't understand is that your commitment is to *interview* all the time, not to *hire* all the time. Chris Burkhard, whom I just described, interviewed someone during layoffs. If he can pull that off, then you can certainly meet with potential employees when you don't have an open position. To do this, you just have to communicate your recruiting approach appropriately and let people know that:

1. You are not actively looking to hire at this time; but
2. You are always interested in meeting great people.
3. Sometimes when you meet the right people, you hire them first and then find a position for them.

4. If you meet them and like them, but don't have a role for them, you are happy to refer them to others in your network who might be helpful in their job search.

I would argue that it is actually preferable to interview when you *don't* have a position open. It makes you more confident and selective in the hiring process. To save time, you can always offer a phone interview to a candidate first and spend 15 minutes reviewing his goals and accomplishments. If you are not impressed, end the call and move on. If you are, bring him in for a face-to-face interview. Again, you can limit the time you invest to 20 to 30 minutes and politely end the interview. This approach works because many strong, growing companies hire great A-players when they meet them, whether they have a spot available or not. A-players often have highly transferable skills and can excel in more than one role.

Carl Gersbach, introduced in Chapter 1, is managing director of Brokerage Services for CB Richard Ellis, Inc. in Philadelphia. Carl is a strong recruiter. He understands that finding A-players means interviewing whether he has a position to fill or not. Carl explains, "We try never to turn down an interview, and during those interviews we educate people about our business. We'll even help them network and reach out to competitors if we have no available positions. We do this because, if and when they become successful, we want them to remember that we treated them well." Even the most talented performers experience a high amount of stress during the job-seeking process. Your willingness to educate them about your industry and introduce them to other company's decision makers will pay off. Anytime you help people get jobs, they remember you with appreciation. These relationships will generate new hires and referrals down the road.

A-Player Principle: You have to *interview* all the time, not hire all the time. With every interview, you develop one more contact who can benefit your company.

Building Your Farm Team

The third step to creating an organization of A-players is to build your farm team, which brings your A-player mind-set and your commitment to interviewing together in one simple system. Major league baseball teams, for instance, don't just hire players off the street; they draft talented college and international players, put them on a minor league "farm team," and then promote the best players to the big leagues when they need them.

In the spring of 1999 (before cell phones became ubiquitous), a major league baseball scout for the Colorado Rockies named Jay Darnell pulled into a truck stop to report on a young player he had recently spotted.[1] He informed his contact at the Rockies' home office that this college player was going to hit for a lot of power in the major leagues one day. But Darnell received no response. The Rockies never pursued the player.

Later that year, this same player—Albert Pujols—got a chance to try out for the Tampa Bay Devil Rays, which also chose not to sign him. Finally, the St. Louis Cardinals drafted Pujols in the thirteenth round of the 1999 draft. Major league scouts will tell you that it is rare to find a superstar in the fifth or sixth round of the draft. To find one in the thirteenth round is essentially unheard of. Albert Pujols was the 402nd overall pick in the baseball draft that year and received a $70,000 bonus—pennies in the world of big-league sports.

Pujols was then assigned to one of the Cardinals' minor league farm teams. In 2001, he was playing well in the minors when the Cardinals' regular third baseman got injured. So Pujols was called up to the big leagues—and he never looked back. He was the 2001 National League Rookie of the Year, won the National League Most Valuable Player title three times, received numerous other awards, and is now mentioned in the same breath as legendary players like Hank Aaron, Mickey Mantle, and Joe DiMaggio. The Cardinals have gone on to compete in two World Series (one of which they won), build a new stadium, and have near-sellout games for years—in large part because of this thirteenth-round pick. All of this happened because the Cardinals—rather than the Rays or the

Rockies—had the foresight to sign a future A-player to their farm team three years before he ever got a big-league hit.

Recruit Before You Need To

The Cardinals already had their backup in Pujols when their third baseman was forced to stop playing. The same should be true for you. In fact, the best way to make hiring mistakes is to start recruiting *when* you have a job to fill. You tend to be in "crisis mode" when you are short staffed, so it is not the ideal time to make a hiring decision. The best way to hire A-players is to find them *before* you need them. Several of my clients have successfully applied the farm team approach to their businesses, and it is paying off in better hires, superior employees, and more effective leadership and management.

Fred Christen is president of Hallmark Stone, a fabricator of natural stone countertops. Fred has used the farm team concept to guarantee that every department in his company, down to the manufacturing floor, is continually staffed with A-players. Fred conducts monthly reviews of the company's "People Bank," an Excel spreadsheet on the company's server. At any point in time, each department manager is required to have two or three candidates entered in the People Bank who have been interviewed, assessed, and drug-tested. The dates of these interviews are recorded on the sheet. The person is ready to be hired but does not yet work for Hallmark Stone. When a position opens up at Hallmark Stone, the manager can give the person a call. If he or she is still available, the person can start immediately (or at least within a couple of weeks).

You can tell that Hallmark Stone is serious about this process because it completely vets job candidates *before* it has an open position. It's an additional expenditure of time and money, but the benefits of this process far outweigh the costs. Instead of engaging in sporadic, reactionary job interviews that can result in poor hires, this company has a consistent, proactive process for finding great people. The time and money spent on interviews, assessments, and drug tests are a worthwhile investment that pays off in a team full of A-players.

Of course, A-players who were available four to six weeks ago might not be available right now. So Hallmark Stone's managers stay in touch with candidates every few weeks or so, keep them informed about the company and receive an update on their status. If people take another position or become otherwise unavailable, the managers must add new people to their farm team. To keep their farm team updated, Hallmark Stone's managers interview one or two candidates each month. These interviews are not an overwhelming time commitment, just a constant part of their schedule.

> **A-Player Principle:** By developing a farm team of A-players, you require the leaders of your company to refresh their pool of qualified talent continually. This prevents your company from hiring out of desperation.

Should You Advertise for Your Farm Team?

How in the world do you advertise for job candidates if you don't have a job to fill? For the most part, you don't. Companies find people for their farm teams through referrals, not job postings. Employees and others involved with the company have an A-player mind-set and provide a constant flow of referrals. That eliminates problems that would arise from running a job announcement without a position to fill. At the same time, if a department's farm team is small and there is an upcoming need for new employees, the company will post the job online. Doing this creates a spike in the amount of time that must be dedicated to reviewing resumes and interviewing candidates. However, the basic interviewing process remains the same.

Every Manager Has a Farm Team

One of the simple yet brilliant elements of the farm team approach is that recruiting becomes the job of every leader in your company.

Each manager has a farm team "quota" for which he or she is held accountable. As a result, every company leader recognizes and owns the importance of recruiting all the time. If you believe that what gets measured gets done, then put an objective like this in place for your department heads today. You empower your managers when you give them a recruiting goal like this, because you communicate that you trust their instincts and want them looking for great people to add to the team. You must lead the recruiting process, but you don't have to do it alone.

> **A-Player Principle:** What gets measured gets done. Hold your managers responsible for having at least two "live" candidates on their farm team at any one time. This makes recruiting *our* problem rather than just *your* problem.

Explain the Farm Team Approach to Job Candidates Up Front

Explain your farm-team system to job candidates right away. Don't take them through the entire procedure—including on-line assessments or a drug test—only to tell them that you don't have a job to fill. Instead, explain that:

1. Your company is committed to building a great team rather than just filling positions.
2. As a result, you interview people all the time and are always looking for A-players.
3. When you find a great person, you hire him or her immediately if you can or you put the person on your farm team and stay in touch until something becomes available. Alternatively, if nothing works out at your company, you may be able to help him or her find a job with another company.

As long as you make people aware of your plans right off the bat, you won't have any problems. I actually believe that this kind of approach *attracts* A-players to your company, because people will respect your commitment to finding the best talent for your team. They will want to be part of a company with this kind of focus and dedication.

The Power of Staying in Touch

Let's say that you put a candidate on your farm team who is between jobs. Although you stay in touch, he takes another job before you can hire him. *Don't lose contact.* Put him on your e-mail list, and flag his record along with other similar contacts. Send out quarterly "checking-in" e-mails with updates on your department or your company. I don't care if you include these people on your personal Christmas card list; figure out a way to keep in touch.

A-players don't just work for companies, they work for *people.* If you maintain a personal connection with people and remind them that you are around, it will pay off in quality hires, referrals, and new business down the road. Every professional recruiter will tell you that "A-players refer A-players." If you stay in touch with great individuals, they will help you to build your A-player team— whether you end up hiring them or not.

Another reason to preserve communication with A-players is that they may still come to work for you if their new role is not a good fit. The fact is, it can be hard for A-players to find a good home. Earlier in my career, I served as an executive recruiter placing financial executives. I once was trying to find a position for a young woman who was a rising star at a large public accounting firm. She had been promoted quickly, showed strong leadership talents, passed the CPA exam on the first sitting, had a 4.0 undergraduate grade point average, and was a model in her spare time. (No one says life is fair.)

I called the local affiliate of a major TV network to market this woman as a job candidate. I described her background and told the vice president of finance that she was in high demand. It has been well over a decade since he gave me his reply, but I remember it to this day. "Eric," he said, "you and I both know that there are not that many companies out there that are a good fit for a *real* A-player." In other words, A-players often find it difficult to connect with an employer that offers the pay, challenge, development opportunities, and career path they want in a job. The VP of finance was right.

So keep in contact with A-players, even if they take a job with someone else. They may come back to you if they find their new employer is really an employer for B or C-players.

A-Player Principle: There are not that many great companies and challenging jobs for A-players, so stay in touch with every A-player you meet. Sooner or later, some of those people will come back to you.

The Secret to Dealing with Poor Performers

If you require your managers to develop a farm team for their departments, you receive a powerful additional benefit: your company will get better at dealing with poor performance and inadequate performers. Here's how.

I once worked with a consulting firm that had a poor performer in a key role. This individual had a chip on his shoulder, overvalued his own abilities, consistently missed deadlines, and was difficult to work with. The leaders and senior managers of this firm did everything to try to turn this guy around: coaching, in-your-face performance reviews, more focused job descriptions, increased handholding on projects. Nothing really worked, yet it took them three years to fire him. Why? Because they did not have anyone to take his place. He was experienced enough to do some things well. Even though he detracted from the firm's performance in a number of ways, he was the proverbial "warm body" that was better than no body at all.

When your managers have a farm team, they have options. This makes them more courageous and direct—especially with your prodding—in dealing with subpar performance. Face it: most people act in their own self-interest. If your department managers don't have a farm team, they'll hang onto poor performers to avoid creating more work for themselves by firing them. Furthermore, there are no guarantees that they will find someone *good* to take their place on short notice. So your managers complain to you and try to coach their poor performers. You all trudge ahead. Nothing changes.

A good farm team transforms all this. It allows department managers to call up their A-players at any time. Since these people will be available for only a brief window of time, it is in the managers' best interest to deal quickly with poor performers by being direct, providing accountability, and then replacing people if necessary with candidates from their farm team.

This is how better recruiting begets more effective leadership and management. Take a moment to estimate the number of chronic poor performers you have in your company. Consider the impact that having more courage to deal with poor performance would have on your business. Your whole organization will improve if you establish a great farm team program.

> **A-Player Principle:** A great farm team will make your managers more courageous in dealing with poor performance and poor performers.

Employee Referrals

You build a farm team based on your network and referrals first, with job postings and advertisements used to supplement this flow of candidates. Employee referrals are absolutely necessary to any farm team's success. As a means of encouraging this, Hallmark Stone offers staff members a $250 bonus for every person they refer who is ultimately hired. Many other companies use some form of employee referral bonus, some quite generous. I know a senior consultant who was surprised to receive a $7,000 referral check one day. He had referred a contact to his employer six months before and then had forgotten all about it. That check made him start paying attention! Companies pay recruiters 20 to 30 percent of first-year starting salaries to fill one position. Any referral fee you pay for a quality employee is going to be a terrific bargain compared to this. The next sections present a few key points to make these kinds of programs flourish.

Referrals Wanted—Always

The best way to get employees to refer high-quality people to your company is to interview constantly. (Is this starting to sound familiar?) Going to your employees twice per year and asking for referrals to fill an open position is a low-percentage play. You'll know you're doing it right when, unprompted, you hear your employees tell their contacts, "You should talk to our company. We're interviewing all the time." Your employees are just like you: busy. If you want them to focus on discovering great potential employees, you have to keep them aware of your program at all times and consistently remind them how much the company values their referrals.

By and large, people love to play and win games. A referral bonus is a smart investment because it turns the employee referral process into a game that employees can win. These programs are not first and foremost about the money but rather about employees who take pride in their company and want to help make it better. So by all means, do include this kind of bonus program in your company. But when you talk about it, don't just discuss it in terms of the reward. Focus on the fact that it enhances your current employees' opportunity to keep the company growing by continually adding A-players to the team.

Develop an Internal Farm Team

As your company grows, you will have the opportunity to develop an internal farm team by incubating your own talent. Take, for example, RSI Kitchen & Bath, a full-service kitchen and bath design and remodeling company headquartered in St. Louis, Missouri, with offices across the state. RSI has found that one of the best ways to find A-player staff members is to grow its own talent. The company employs two kinds of salespeople: inside showroom salespeople who work with consumers, and outside salespeople who work with developers on new home construction and other commercial projects. While an inside salesperson focuses on individual kitchen and bath remodels, outside salespeople work on projects that can include hundreds of new homes. To be an outside salesperson, you have to have very strong sales skills and unquestionable technical knowledge about kitchen and bath design and construction.

RSI has found that it takes salespeople years to acquire the level of technical knowledge required to sell large projects. As a result, the company generally promotes its own inside salespeople to be outside salespeople. In addition to being an important role in and of itself, the inside sales role is a talent incubator for the outside sales role. RSI has created a farm team within its own four walls, something that all smart, fast-growing companies should do. It provides a pool of known talent from which to draw, and it ensures that the people you hire already support your culture and values.

Do you have a position in your company that is—or can be turned into—a talent incubator? Do you have a system for developing and promoting the best people in this position? Do you emphasize to both current and potential employees that this career path exists for A-players? All these steps will help your company to serve as its own talent incubator.

> **A-Player Principle:** As your company grows, look for opportunities to develop a farm team within your own company. These people are a known entity—they have proven skills and already share your values.

Building Your Brand to Attract A-Players

Google receives more than 20,000 resumes a week—two resumes every minute.[2] In terms of hiring A-players—well, these people often come *to* Google. While the company does actively pursue

A-players, it can focus on a rigorous process for weeding people out during the interview process, hire those that fit Google's A-Player Profile, and then work assiduously to retain them.

While Google is a premier example of the power of a brand in recruiting, it is by no means the only company that is able to appeal to a strong pool of potential employees. Tracy Moore is vice president of human resources for HOK, one of the premier architectural firms in the world. HOK works hard to differentiate itself as the best place to work for world's top architects, and it has no trouble attracting job applicants. Tracy gets three to five unsolicited calls every day from recruiters who want to place candidates with her company, but she does not need them. HOK receives hundreds of qualified applications each year because it has such a powerful brand.

Great brands attract A-players. While you might have yet to achieve the same kind of name recognition as Google and HOK, there are ways in which your company stands out from your competition. Determine exactly what these stand-out factors are and develop your brand in these areas. A great reputation as a company that provides superior service, or gives back to the community, or develops terrific leaders will fascinate potential employees just as it attracts customers. Cultivating your brand and your reputation will help you to attract A-players.

Create a Great First Impression

Don't overlook the first impression that people receive when they initially step into your business. Your office's waiting area, for example, can be designed to communicate the specific messages that your customers and A-player job candidates are hungry to hear. Cenero is a fast-growth, Philadelphia-based company in the audiovisual design, installation, and events industry. In the lobby, Chief Executive Rob Gilfillan literally broadcasts the messages he wants customers and job candidates to see and hear on flat-screen monitors. The monitors prominently display a graph of the company's growth over the past decade. In addition, framed letters from nonprofit organizations express thanks to the company for its contribution of audio-video equipment for underresourced schools. Cenero's lobby is that of a company that is going places. It impresses everyone who walks in with the growth of the company, its values as a community member, and its involvement in cutting-edge audio-visual projects. Before a job candidate or customer ever meets with a Cenero employee, Rob and his company manage to create a fantastic first impression. Why wouldn't potential job candidates want to explore working for this company? What steps can *you* take to improve your company's first impression to visitors?

Authenticity Is Attractive

Developing and communicating a brand in recruiting does not have to be expensive. Often you can differentiate yourself and your company in the eyes of A-players simply by how you act. One of my favorite examples of this occurred when I referred a 25-year-old salesman as a job applicant to Jeff Phillips, the president of Fleet Feet Inc. This salesman was working for a large corporation and felt stifled by the bureaucracy. He and Jeff had a good initial phone conversation and agreed to meet at a coffee shop near Fleet Feet's headquarters in Carrboro, North Carolina, for a face-to-face interview. Jeff told him, "I will be the guy wearing shorts and riding a Harley." Here was this gifted young guy who felt stifled in a big corporate environment, and he was going to meet with the president of a company who *wore shorts and rode a motorcycle* to an interview! Jeff was being absolutely authentic, but he was also being intentional. He knew this young sales guy would likely respond very positively to the laid-back, we-don't-take-ourselves-too-seriously culture of Fleet Feet. He made sure that he communicated this nonverbal message to this candidate, and it worked.

Attract A-Players by Serving the Community

Big Shark Bicycle on St. Louis' Delmar Loop is a bike shop that serves the community by promoting and directing races across the city. Every Tuesday night in the spring and summer, Mike Weiss and his crew put on a training criterium (a bike race on a closed course) for everyone from elite racers to beginners to develop their road-racing skills. While many races are expensive to enter and require getting up early on a weekend morning, this race is affordable and conducted after working hours, when many riders are available. The evening not only becomes a great chance to practice racing skills, but an opportunity for local cyclists to ride with their friends and meet other members of the cycling community. Cyclists love it; and they love Big Shark for putting it on.

Other bike shops have tried and failed to duplicate Big Shark's success. What makes Big Shark different is that it really *is* committed to making a contribution to others. The events that the company sponsors go beyond competition. They bring people with common interests together and give them a reason to hang out. As a result, the company has developed a strong bond with members of the cycling community.

This bond shows up in Big Shark's recruiting results. Big Shark's A-Player Profile emphasizes that employees should be knowledgeable about cycling and motivated to use this knowledge to serve customers and the community. Because people in the cycling community know Big Shark, they refer service-oriented job candidates to the company. The service-oriented expertise of Big Shark's salespeople then earns the trust of customers—and this trust translates into great customer loyalty and strong sales. For Big Shark, this service-oriented formula has built a successful business.

> **A-Player Principle:** Attract A-players by building an authentic brand. Let people experience the passion behind your business. This will build your reputation and attract employees who share your values.

Keep It On

These strategies for finding A-players and building an A-player team are proven. They work. Apply them to your company and *stick with them.*

Fred Silverman was a legendary television producer in the 1970s who was responsible for shows like *Happy Days* and *Laverne & Shirley*. When asked to explain his strategy for turning a good show into a hit, he had a three-word answer: "Keep it on." Silverman's approach was to create a show that he believed in, put it and keep it on the air, and let the audience find it.

The same approach is true with finding and hiring A-players. You have to implement these strategies and stick with them. Much like finding new customers, this is not an overnight process. Over time you will develop a reputation as an employer of choice. You will also become adept at understanding the profile of people who excel in your environment and hiring them when you find them, even if you have to *create* a position. As you build a team of A-players that out-executes the competition, you will create the business you have always envisioned.

A-Player Payoff Points

Chapter 3: Three Steps to Creating an A-Player Team

- Build a farm team of A-players who work for other companies but want to work for you. This is the pipeline of talent from which to build your company.
- Hiring is a numbers game. Set goals for yourself and your managers as to the number of people you will interview each month. Require all managers to have at least two live candidates on their farm team at all times, which will force them always to be interviewing.
- Remember that constantly interviewing does not mean constantly *hiring.* Develop a reputation as a good person for A-players to meet during their job search.
- Create a talent incubator within your own business. It will become a pool of people who already support your mission and share your values.

- It is ultimately your reputation and brand that attract A-players to your company. Don't keep the advantages of working at your company a secret.
- Your values as an organization are the qualities that differentiate you in A-players' eyes. Let people experience the passion behind your business.

4

Right under Your Nose: Leveraging People You Already Know

I hope you've begun to determine exactly what *kind* of talent you need by honing in on the A-Player Profile for key roles in your company. You have also embarked on creating an A-player mind-set about your team both inside and outside your organization. Now you have to find the right people to hire.

The first step is to reach out to your existing network. Envision your network as a series of concentric circles with your closest relationships at the center and people with whom you are less connected in the successive outward circles. (See Figure 4.1.) Each of these circles contains potential A-player hires and referral sources. Let's first focus on the "bull's-eye" of this circle—people you already know to whom no introduction is required. Members of this group would be glad to take a call or receive an e-mail from you.

It's likely that over time, at least some of the individuals in this group have developed some pretty impressive resumes. Perhaps a friend from elementary school is an officer with a Fortune 500 company, or a contact you made through volunteer work runs a successful, privately-held company. Your roommate from college might be

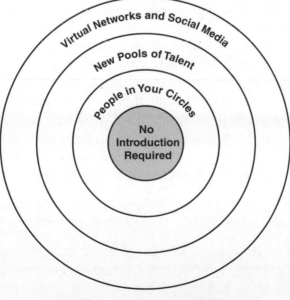

FIGURE 4.1   Sources of A-Players

a successful sales executive. Pay increasing attention to your peers as your career advances. I've observed that sometime in their thirties or early forties, businesspeople become aware that they are now building a network to sustain them through the rest of their careers. Your contemporaries are an essential part of this long-term network. You're at the same place in life, and your careers are (roughly) in the same place. These people are the hub of your professional network—and the core of your effort to find A-players.

Developing a network is much more like cultivating a garden than going out and hunting down dinner. If you want your network to provide you with value in the form of A-player employees, clients, and contacts, then you have to invest time in it. My personal rule is to schedule at least one meeting per week with people in my network or with individuals I want to add to it. Different cities and regions can vary in this regard. My home turf—Philadelphia and the surrounding region—is advanced networking ground. Everyone recognizes the importance of building a network. People know that networking is like investing; you have to make deposits in order to get returns.

Ryan Lafferty—a partner in the retained search firm Attolon Partners—points out that chief executive officers of substantial business enterprises are inevitably strong relationship builders. They have been successful at developing ties with people throughout their careers and habitually call on those relationships when they reach the top job in order to establish an organization of highly talented people. They know that their businesses cannot thrive on the efforts of a single person. Their network becomes a key to their success. So when I ask you to make cultivating your network a continuous focus in your career, what I am *really* asking you to do is start thinking and acting like the most successful CEOs.

Friends and Family

I have never heard a piece of advice more widely given and more extensively ignored than "Never hire friends or family." This can be tough advice to follow, particularly for those just starting a business—friends and family may be the only people you can persuade to join you! I work with a number of companies in which multiple family members play important roles. Entire books have been written on running family businesses, but there is one key principle relative to recruiting and hiring: don't hire people because they are friends or family members, but don't overlook people for that same reason.

When John F. Kennedy was elected president of the United States, his father, Joe Kennedy Sr., insisted that Bobby Kennedy, the president's younger brother, be named attorney general. John Kennedy resisted the idea because he did not want to be accused of nepotism, but his father's desires prevailed, and Bobby was appointed to the position. Early on during the Kennedy presidency, the Bay of Pigs debacle occurred. The administration had encouraged a group of Central Intelligence Agency–backed Cuban fighters to invade Fidel Castro's Cuba and then left them to perish when the surprise attack failed. Though Kennedy was severely criticized by politicians and citizens alike, his brother was his staunchest ally during that difficult period. John Kennedy reflected afterward, "Now I see that Dad was right. Bobby is the only one that I can trust."[1] In the same way, a close friend or family member could become *your* most trusted A-player.

A-players come from all sorts of different sources. If you know a terrific person from your own clan or with whom you have been friends since kindergarten, don't reject out of hand the possibility of hiring him or her. Instead, treat that working relationship the same way you would any other: Define roles and responsibilities before you make any hiring decisions. Agree on the financial compensation and *absolutely* put it in writing. State, up front, how you will exit this working relationship if things don't work out. Handled right, strong people with personal ties to you can be the foundation of a fantastic team.

In addition, don't forget your A-player mind-set when it comes to your family and friends. Educate them about the person you want to hire. One of these close contacts may well refer your next A-player employee.

> **A-Player Principle:** Don't hire people because they are friends or family, but don't overlook them because of their close connection either.

Your Customers

Often your customers share your passion, something that becomes an important factor in customers becoming A-player employees. Ed and Ellen Griffin own a Fleet Feet Sports franchise in Syracuse, New York, a running specialty store that caters to runners and others who are passionate about fitness. While you don't have to be an elite athlete to work for the company, an enthusiasm for fitness certainly helps. Four times a year, Fleet Feet Syracuse publicizes job openings in an electronic newsletter that goes out to 14,000 people—many of whom are customers. These e-letters are always variations on the same message:

- We're growing!
- We need more great employees.
- If you possess an interest in helping people, an interest in fitness, and the availability to work nights and weekends, please talk to us about a career at Fleet Feet.

The fact that Fleet Feet Syracuse spells out its A-Player Profile in its e-mail blast not only elicits job applicants, it also encourages people to forward the newsletter to others who are interested in running and fitness.

Your employees are one of your company's key connections to many of your customers. So why not give them a process for identifying and recruiting customers who could become your next set of A-players? Every retail floor salesperson at Fleet Feet Syracuse is trained to assess whether one of their customers could be a good fit as an employee. It is not unusual for a retail floor associate to spend 30 to 45 minutes fitting a customer with the right shoes, clothes, and other products. An employee can learn a lot about a customer during those 45 minutes.

If a salesperson has a good feeling about a customer based on the company's A-Player Profile, the employee is trained to say: "We have a fast-growing business here at Fleet Feet Sports and are always looking for good people. If you know someone who may be interested in talking with us about the opportunities here, please let us know." Then the employee provides the customer with the staff manager's business card. In response to this low-key approach, customers often express personal interest right away or get back in touch within a few days of their visit to the store. From there, they fill out an application to determine if an interview should be scheduled.

Fleet Feet Syracuse provides another example of the tie between marketing and recruiting. The customer acquisition engine at this store is always running, and it fuels the store's recruiting efforts as well. The store acquires 140 to 160 new customers per week on average, more than half of whom subscribe to the newsletter. Many of these recently acquired customers are the ones who respond to the company's career opportunities. Sometimes the excitement that new customers feel when they find a high-quality running store makes them want to apply to be a part of it. In other situations, people are new transplants to the area, have a passion for running and fitness, and need a job. Either way, the company is able to make their existing customer acquisition infrastructure serve double duty as a recruiting system. Fleet Feet Syracuse therefore spends very little additional money to build its farm team and find more A-player employees.

A-Player Principle: Use your existing customer acquisition tools to attract more A-player employees. This requires minimal out-of-pocket expense and puts the return on investment of your recruiting efforts through the roof.

Turning Customers Down

You don't want to lose a customer in the process of recruiting and evaluating him or her for employment. The key here is to be extremely clear from the very beginning about the realities of the position. Give people plenty of opportunities to disqualify themselves from the role once they understand what's really involved. Let them know that you value them too much to hire them if you don't think it will be a good experience for everyone involved. People who have never worked in your industry, for example, may be passionate about the focus of your business (fitness, technology, media, or the like) but might not want to turn that passion into a real job with all the requirements that go along with it. In other situations, customers may not be able or willing to work the kind of hours that a position with your company requires. List the negatives as well as the positives of the job early on in the recruiting process. Tell customers that if a job with you is not the right fit, you will help them connect with other companies that would be good for them. Be clear and direct with every applicant about the position's requirements. This helps you to reduce misunderstandings and bad hires in general—and particularly with customers.

Use a "Soft" Approach to Recruiting Customers

When the employees of Fleet Feet Syracuse approach a customer about working for the company, they use a classic recruiters' line that I recommend to you as well: "If you know anyone who is interested in working for us, we would love to talk with them." What they are really asking is "Are *you* interested in working for us?" This is a soft, non-offensive way to recruit. People don't want to be hounded, but they do want to be *wanted*. Take this low-key approach to recruiting, and don't get your feelings hurt if people are initially uninterested. It often takes months (even years) to recruit an A-player. But the wait is well worth it.

Have a Simple Employment Application Process

Have a straightforward job application process in place and make sure your employees understand it. It's one thing to spot great candidates, but you have to get them to *apply* for a job in order to hire them. The process can be as simple as the five steps outlined next.

1. Get to know customers or other people and determine whether they match up with your A-Player Profile.
2. If you think they do, tell them about your company's growth and resulting employment opportunities. Talk about your A-Player Profile, then ask if they know anyone who might be interested in such an opportunity.
3. If they are personally interested, provide them with the business card of the manager or human resources person to contact.
4. Have them fill out an employment application in person or online.
5. Schedule an initial phone screen or interview.

If your people don't understand the employment application process or find it to be a hassle, they are more apt to ignore opportunities to recruit potential A-players.

Treat Everyone Well

Make sure that everyone who applies for a job is treated well. This means that you communicate with them, keep them updated on your process, and talk with them early in the interview process about who is and is not a good fit for your company. If your employees don't have confidence that you will treat their customers respectfully, they are not going to refer them to you for employment.

A-Player Principle: Your customers often share your passion and can be great A-player employees. Establish a simple process for appropriately recruiting customers. Then overcommunicate during the interview process with the people you recruit to avoid bad feelings if you don't hire them.

Customers as Referral Sources

You may not hire your clients, but if you know how to ask, they can be a terrific referral source for A-players. Make sure you communicate your A-player mind-set to your customers. If they know you're always looking for talent, they will refer their friends and colleagues. The fact that you are always interviewing also communicates your commitment to delivering an exceptional customer experience. More A-players at your company means an increasingly valuable experience for your clients.

There are some specific programs which you can put in place to encourage your salespeople to ask customers for A-player referrals. Many large, sales-driven organizations like the Northwestern Mutual Financial Network and CB Richard Ellis are moving to a team-driven sales model. Instead of hiring new salespeople, giving them a cubicle and a phone, and wishing them "good luck," these organizations hire A-players as sales assistants and assign them to established producers. This increases the chances that young salespeople will make it in the business and frees up successful reps to prospect for bigger deals.

This kind of sales assistant program creates a powerful incentive for your top-producing salespeople to recruit less-experienced A-players as their assistants. When top salespeople are hiring assistants for themselves, they take the recruiting very seriously. They ask everyone they know, including their clients, for A-player referrals. In response, their clients know that the opportunity to work as an assistant for a top producer is a great one, so they feel good about referring A-players. The result for your company is a strong pipeline of talent that pays off today and tomorrow. This is a powerful approach. How can you apply it to your organization?

A-Player Principle: Educate your customers about your A-player mind-set. They will refer talented people to you and feel great about your commitment to building the best team to serve them.

Your Vendors

I know a top-producing salesperson who used to sell copiers and other business machines. At one of the offices he called on, he struck up a relationship with the receptionist. They started dating and ended up getting married. He then took a sales position with this same business. (His new wife's family owned it.)

You don't literally have to bring A-players into your family in order to recruit them. But your suppliers' people are a prime hunting ground for your recruiting efforts. For example, it is common practice for corporations to recruit attorneys from the law firms that serve them. While law firms don't want to lose their best people, they also understand that, handled correctly, their relationship with the client will be stronger by having one of their alumni working there. The same thing goes for your CPA firm, your advertising agency, and the other vendors that serve your business. All of them employ people who are potential A-players for your business. Generally, the biggest challenge in interviewing and hiring is that you have never worked with the people you are considering for hire, but that's not the case with your vendors' employees. You work with them every day and know how they operate under pressure.

> **A-Player Principle:** You work with people from your vendors every day. Focus on recruiting the best of them into your organization.

Create an A-Player Target List

You should always have a target list of two or three people who work for your competitors whom you would love to have working for you. These will most likely be seasoned executives, managers, and salespeople who would make an immediate positive impact if they came to work for you. I recently met with the head of sales for a major corporation. We talked about recruiting and hiring, and he said, "I am not hiring today unless your name is Jim Richards or Sandra Jones." These are not their actual names, but he did know by name the people he wanted to hire that day, despite a company-wide hiring freeze. That is the kind of targeted approach that creates an A-player team.

Don't wait to cultivate these relationships. It is a long-term process to move a big hitter from one organization to another. Once you have people on your target list, find mutual contacts who can help you to schedule a meeting. Who are your common friends? Who can help to set up an introductory lunch? Even if the person on your list is not actively looking for a new role, effective business-people know that they have to take responsibility for their own careers. The best employment situation in the world can change into a nightmare through an acquisition, divestiture, or change in corporate strategy. As a result, people typically are open to this kind of meeting as long as it is discreet, low-key, and focused on building relationships as opposed to making immediate commitments.

I have a friend who calls this kind of activity "threading the needle." To recruit someone, you first get a relationship started, figuratively passing the thread through the eye of the needle. As you get to know people and understand their goals, challenges, hopes, and fears, you work the needle down the thread. You develop a real relationship that can turn into, among other things, an A-player hire. Can you name one A-player with whom you are threading the needle today?

> **A-Player Principle:** "Thread the needle" with A-players. Lay the relational groundwork today that will help you recruit your competitors' best people tomorrow.

Don't Make Up People's Minds for Them

One of the ways that recruiting is like sales is that you never know who will say yes—so you always have to give your prospects the opportunity to buy. This is particularly true when it comes to hiring

A-players away from your competitors or other successful companies. Rich Ledbetter, chief operating officer of Castle Construction, hired the assistant to the CEO of a multibillion-dollar company simply because he was confident enough to offer her this opportunity. She was at a point in her life and career when she wanted to work for a smaller organization and was ready to make a switch to a company just like his. But he found this out only because he asked. If he had "known" that she would never leave a great role working for a high-powered CEO in a huge company, he would never have made this great hire.

> **A-Player Exercise:** Name one or two dream hires who could make a huge contribution to your business. Schedule some time with them and invite them to work for you. Don't let your jaw hit your chest if they say yes, but don't be depressed if they say no. Whatever happens, commit to staying in touch with these people. You want to be the first person A-players call when they are considering a career move.

Remember that C-Players Often Sell Themselves *Better* than A-Players

If you are reaching out to proven stars in your industry, keep in mind that they often don't sell themselves as well as C-players do. Elaine Hughes, president of New York-based search firm E.A. Hughes & Company, points out that, particularly at senior levels, it is often the B- and C-players who sell themselves the best because they do it a lot. The A-players are not out interviewing and actively seeking their next job because they perform well and get paid good money for their results. At least to start, they are not selling you, you are selling them.

While this does not mean that you should pander, it does mean that you ought to pursue A-players appropriately. Make the case for working for you and your company. What's in it for these people? Why would their careers and lives be better working for you? Don't overdo it, of course; you will likely not bring such a person over to you in a first meeting. If you commit to "threading the needle" with as many A-players as you can, you will find that circumstances will evolve to bring some of them your way. The political landscape may change, or their company may be acquired. They may be passed over for a promotion six months from now. The work environment at their current employer may go downhill because the company hires too many B- and C-players. People change jobs for many reasons. Your responsibility is to be on their radar screen *before* these events occur so that A-players call you first when they start thinking about making a job change.

Internal Hires

Rich Ryffel, managing director for investment banking at Edward Jones, makes the point that you should not neglect internal hires when looking for A-players. While this may seem obvious, the fact is that—regardless of company size—A-players can get stuck in departmental politics that prevent the strongest employees from receiving the best opportunities. Make sure that you don't have weak department heads or team leaders who keep their best people from taking good opportunities within your own organization. If there is one thing that A-players won't abide, it is being limited in their own growth and development. If they can't grow with you, they will grow with another company (quite possibly one of your competitors).

I know a large sales organization that has both wholesale and retail divisions. One day, the two top salespeople from the retail division showed up at the office of the wholesale division's vice president of sales. They asked for a private meeting and then told him that they wanted to move divisions in order to work for him. This kind of move had never been made before, and as you might imagine, it did not engender warm feelings between the heads of the two divisions. But to the CEO's credit, he let it happen. He recognized that if these two top salespeople were willing to make this kind of brazen request and risk their current jobs, they would likely leave the company entirely if they were not accommodated. The sales reps went on to be top producers for the wholesale division because the CEO allowed an internal competition for talent.

> **A-Player Principle:** It does no good to hire A-players if you can't keep them around. The A-players in your company will gravitate to your strongest leaders. Don't fight this dynamic. Instead, challenge the other leaders to do the things necessary to keep their best people around.

The Critical Role of Assistant Manager

I have a number of clients that have multiple chains or offices located across the country. In all of them, the branch manager or store manager plays a critical role. They have profit and loss responsibility. They make hiring and firing decisions, oversee inventory levels, and lead sales and customer service efforts. One of the most important roles to recruit and fill well in organizations like these is the assistant manager role. This "apprentice" learns the business while helping to run it. When a new manager position opens up, the first place that these companies look to fill the job is the ranks of the assistant managers.

Store managers and branch managers in your ranks should be held accountable for recruiting and hiring the best assistant managers possible. Each should be measured on his or her ability to build a farm team of potential assistant managers, to hire the right people into this role, and to develop them into leaders who can run their own operations. You have to appeal to your current managers' self-interest to make this happen. Make it clear to them that their own promotions ride in part on their ability to recruit strong successors. If people's careers are affected by their ability to hire A-players, they will take recruiting seriously. They will develop the A-player mentality that we discuss in this book. Don't take all the responsibility for recruiting A-players on your own back. Make it a corporate priority for which everyone takes ownership.

> **A-Player Principle:** To make hiring A-players a corporate priority, measure and reward your leaders upon their recruiting results. If people have to hire well in order to advance their own careers, they will get focused on finding strong performers.

Turning B-Players into A-Players

While we are on the topic of internal hiring to find A-players, let's address the perennial question of how to turn a B-player into an A-player. Sometimes all a B-player needs is experience and coaching to become a star. There are other situations, however, in which people have been promoted beyond their abilities. What do you do then?

I once watched a Japanese bonsai master demonstrate how to take an immature young tree and make it appear centuries old. The first thing he did was to take this stringy young sapling and cut off its top. He pointed out that in order to make a young tree appear older, you have to reduce its size to give it the proportions of a much older tree. In other words, to make it *appear* bigger, you actually had to make it smaller.

The same is true of B-players: Sometimes you can turn them into A-players by making their jobs smaller. Assign them roles where they can shine. If people have a strong work ethic, drive, and integrity, then they can be A-players—somewhere.

An architectural firm with which I worked had a diligent employee who struggled with multitasking and getting his assignments done quickly. The managing partners wanted this architect to thrive at the firm, so I worked with them to come up with a solution that leveraged his strengths and managed his weaknesses. We put him into a role that played to his detail orientation and desire to coach others. We teamed him up with a senior project manager who had strong client relationship skills. This change limited the scope of his responsibilities. He was always going to play a behind-the-scenes role rather than focus on managing clients. Yet he flourished in this position with its more limited scope. He was not a "rainmaker," but he set the pace within the firm on quality control (a critical issue for such firms) and mentoring younger architects. Within the parameters of his new job, he became an A-player.

> **A-Player Principle:** If people have a good work ethic and possess integrity, they can be an A-player somewhere. Sometimes you can turn these B-players into A-players by making their jobs smaller.

Tapping into the Contacts of New Hires

Every time you hire an A-player, you have the opportunity to tap into a brand-new network of job candidates. Headhunters know this. Every name that's provided to recruiters as a current or past supervisor, peer, subordinate, or reference is another contact to add to their database. The same thing can be true for your company if you handle it right. Take the time to talk to new hires about your A-player mind-set and profile. In the midst of these conversations, ask for their advice on finding great people to fill other roles in your organization. Many times they will volunteer to reach out to people they know who would be a good fit.

Taking Action to Tap into Your Network

In the end, you have to be committed to networking if you are going to hire and create an A-player team. Some of us are natural networkers. It is in our nature to develop relationships and stay in touch with people. For others of us, spending time to develop a network might seem like a waste of time that could be spent on "real work." But finding and hiring A-players absolutely requires a strong system of relationships.

I recently spent two days with a company that is hiring a new salesperson. The president and vice president of operations are both successful businesspeople and great guys, but they will be the first to tell you that their strong suit is operations, not networking. I challenged each of them to schedule a minimum of one lunch meeting or coffee every two weeks that focused on developing and cultivating their business relationships. You have to schedule these meetings intentionally if you want to strengthen your core set of connections so that you can—among other goals—find and hire A-players.

A-Player Payoff Points

Chapter 4: Right under Your Nose: Leveraging People You Already Know

- You have to tap into and cultivate your existing network to find A-players.
- Don't hire people because they are close friends or family members, but don't automatically exclude people because of these close ties either. It can be worth navigating the relational dynamics to hire a true A-player who is already close with you.
- Your customers can be a great source of A-player employees. Teach your employees a process for recruiting customers that is appropriate and effective.
- To avoid hurt feelings and lost business down the road, be very clear up front about the requirements of a job with all job applicants. Let people know that you will only hire them if you are convinced your company can provide a long-term career in which they can thrive.
- Develop a sales assistant program for your top salespeople, and have your salespeople recruit their own assistants. To

get the best person for this position, salespeople will tap into their own client base and their short list of quality contacts.

- Look to your vendors for A-players who already understand your business.
- Develop a target list of A-players who work for your competitors, and cultivate these relationships. Hiring just one of these people can be a game-changer for your business.
- If you know someone who would be a terrific addition to your team, have the courage to say so and ask him or her to come to work for you.
- Remember that C-players often sell themselves better than A-players. You need to be willing to pursue A-players and cultivate relationships with them over time. They will yield fruit down the road.
- Don't be afraid of moving A-players between bosses, departments, or divisions. That is one important strategy for keeping the A-players that you already have.
- Turn B-players into A-players by tightening the focus of their roles. Sometimes the best way to turn people into A-players is to make their jobs *smaller*.
- A newly hired A-player has a brand-new network to tap into. Get new hires engaged in your A-player mind-set quickly and ask them to tap into their networks for more high-caliber people.
- Schedule two networking meetings (one-on-one or large group) into your schedule each month. These meetings will pay off in A-player hires, new clients, and expanded personal and professional opportunities.

5

Don't Just Sit There. Reach Out!

everaging your existing relationships, while essential, is not enough to keep your pipeline full of A-player prospects. You must continually expand your contacts in order to find and hire more A-players. While you typically don't have to do much more networking than you already are doing to find these people, identifying and connecting with A-players must become a focus of all your networking activities.

Recruiter in Chief

I once spoke to a group of about 100 engineers for a local trade association. Though the average age of the attendees was thirty, at one table sat a man in his fifties who stood out for both his polish and his confidence. I met him after my program and he introduced himself as Robert. He owned an engineering consulting firm in the region. I said to him, "Robert, I am looking around and this room is not exactly filled with your peers. Why are you here?" He looked

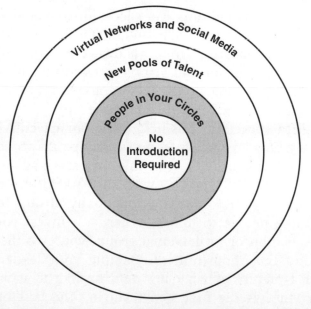

FIGURE 5.1   Sources of A-Players: People in Your Circles

right at me and immediately gave me this answer: "That's simple. I am recruiter in chief for my company."

As recruiter in chief for your company, you own the responsibility for identifying A-players and bringing them to your team. Robert made himself available to the members of this engineering group as a leader and mentor in order to build his farm team. He did not actively recruit everyone he met or hand out business cards after my program. But he understood the power and importance of building relationships with A-players *before* they were looking for a new place to work. He made connections with the seasoned youth in this group and tapped into a pool of potential A-players. Taking a leadership role in the group and showing up at the meetings gave him an opportunity to get to know these younger engineers over time. He was constantly interviewing people—whether they knew it or not. Over time, these contacts grew into strong relationships, which in turn generated some great new hires.

Running with the Big Dogs

A-players have big aspirations. They look for role models, people I call "Big Dogs," whom they can emulate and follow. Robert was a Big Dog in this engineering group. He owned his company and had 50 employees working for him. Everyone else in the room was collecting a W-2. The younger engineers wanted to get to know him in part because they wanted to be like him one day.

If you are a successful business owner or executive, you are already a Big Dog in the professional groups in which you participate. Whether you know it or not, you serve as a role model for ambitious people. A-players want to work for strong leaders, but unfortunately there are not that many strong leaders out there for these people to follow. When you invest your time in a trade association or professional group, you give the A-players in the group the opportunity to sample your leadership style and to get a picture of what it would be like to work for you. That experience is the first step in hiring the best of them for your company.

> **A-Player Principle:** People want to follow the Big Dogs in their industry. If you have been successful, take the time to give back to business and professional groups. The A-players you meet will make this time investment pay off.

Industry Conferences and Continuing Education

Several years ago, I was talking with the partners of a civil engineering firm about strategies for creating an A-player team. They mentioned that they hated sending their top employees to the continuing education classes that were required in their industry. At these classes, their best employees rubbed shoulders with executives from the competition, and some of these relationships inevitably resulted in job offers. The recruiters in chief from these competitive firms were out in force—and this firm was sending their best employees right into their sights.

While you usually can't pull your employees out of these events, you can turn them to your advantage. Get everyone in your business who participates in these events focused on identifying and connecting with A-players. If you don't talk up the importance of this relationship building, most of your people will never give it a second thought. Remember your A-player mind-set, and remind everyone that these events are full of A-players who could be big contributors to your company. Starting on the morning of the first session and continuing the length of the event, your team should be on the lookout for the next addition to your company. I don't care if you are tired after a day of boring lectures—go to the bar with everyone and hang out. You are just one conversation away from finding your next A-player.

This does *not* mean that you or your people should be aggressive recruiters at these events. In fact, it's just the opposite. Adopt a laid-back attitude with everyone you meet and avoid mentioning employment opportunities at your company. Just connect with people, get to know them, and learn about their areas of expertise. Add them to your contact database and include good notes about your conversation in their record. Send them a good-to-meet-you e-mail once you are back in the office. In the following months, give them a follow-up call just to stay connected. When appropriate, you can even tell them about an open position at your firm and ask, "Who do you know?" Don't be aggressive; be intentional. If you develop and cultivate enough of these connections, you will add some terrific people to your farm team.

> **A-Player Principle:** Industry events and continuing education sessions are filled with A-players. I don't care how boring the seminars are, you have to attend. At the end of the day, socialize with other session participants and find some top prospects for your farm team.

A Note on Recruiting Salespeople

If you are in the market for salespeople, you can plug into almost any professional association or trade group and find happy hunting. Salespeople populate these groups because they are always looking for prospects. While many of them are not good enough to hire, the top one or two salespeople at these events would make a fantastic contribution to any team. When you get involved in the leadership of a trade group that holds some interest for you, it's always a good idea to get to know the salespeople who regularly attend. If, over time, you become impressed with someone's sales approach and results, make sure that they know you are always interested in talking about career development with A-players.

When it comes to hiring salespeople, first look for great sales skills and work ethic. While you can always educate someone on your products and industry, it is much more difficult to teach people how to sell. I know a plumbing distribution company that has had great success in hiring former car salesmen and training them to sell their products. Another company in the sales incentive industry tried mightily to recruit salespeople from their competitors because they thought industry experience was so crucial. Yet their top two salespeople had no industry experience before coming to the company. The lesson: Find great salespeople no matter their background. They will pay off for you.

> **A-Player Principle:** Typically you can teach a great salesperson the technical aspects of your industry. Never drop great salespeople from your farm team just because they don't have experience in your industry.

Stay until the Quesadillas Are Scorched

Professional associations, industry conferences, networking events—you are likely already attending such groups. You don't have to engage in much more networking than you already are to find A-players, but you *do* have to make the networking you're doing pay off. Some people are natural networkers who thrive on meeting new people. I recently went to my wife's twentieth high school reunion. Among the people I met that night was a friend of hers named Matthew who works in business development for an advertising firm in New York City. At about 11 p.m., I glanced around the room, and there was Matthew, laughing and talking with a bunch of people at the bar not associated with our group. He was standing in a room full of old friends and was having a great time making new friends as well. To people like Matthew, a stranger is just friend they haven't met yet. They can't get enough of networking events, and they typically know how to get results out of them.

While I've developed into a strong networker, I'm no Matthew—I have to work at it. If you're like I am, use my number-one principle for making the networking you are already doing pay off: stay until the quesadillas are scorching. At networking events, the appetizers are usually set out in silver chafing dishes with little cans of Sterno beneath them warming the food. You already made the effort to show up at this event. Now you have to stay until the last of the quesadillas are scorched to the bottom of the pan and are about to burst into flame. The best conversations inevitably happen at the end of these events, not at the beginning.

Most networking events follow the same pattern. You arrive, grab a drink, and work the room. Everyone is talking to one person while their eyes rove around trying to locate other people they know. The crowd and music are so loud that you can hear only one word out of three that anyone says. Then you sit down to a mediocre dinner and listen to a speaker who is average at best. As soon as the program is over, 50 percent of the crowd hightails it for the door. Believe it or not, the best part of the evening has just begun. When the crowd diminishes, people relax and feel like they have accomplished what they came to do. Now is the time to strike up a conversation and make a valuable addition to your network. Instead of scanning the room for someone more important to talk to, people can take a few minutes for real back-and-forth. Ask questions about them and their businesses. Take an interest in what they have to say. The best networking connections happen on the way *out* of this kind of event, so keep your eyes on those quesadillas!

> **A-Player Principle:** Stay at networking events until the bitter end. The best conversations often happen during the last 30 minutes.

The Difference between a Contact and a Business Card

I recently helped a company in commercial heating and air conditioning hire a new salesman and implement a sales management process to make sure that he produces for the company. In addition to setting financial goals, we set activity goals for this salesman (i.e., how many phone calls should he make each day, how many networking contacts should he make each week). I made the point to the owner that you have to be careful about giving someone a goal to make "10 new contacts per week via networking events." There is nothing easier, yet less valuable, than going to a networking event and amassing a collection of business cards. To me, new contacts are people you get to know well enough that they take your follow-up call and schedule a face-to-face meeting. If you can't accomplish that, you don't have new contacts; you just have names on a pile of card stock.

Don't Wallow in the Shallow End of the Networking Pool

Consider these two members of a business association or professional group. Networker A attends a few meetings, misses a few others, and otherwise is uninvolved in the group. Networker B attends every meeting and joins the membership committee. Guess which one is going to uncover more A-players and find more business opportunities? Networker B, without question. If you want to get the most that membership in any group has to offer, you have to get deeply involved.

My family and I attend a great church in Philadelphia. It is not particularly prestigious, nor is it frequented by a lot of movers and shakers from the business community. But it is a good fit for our family, and we are very involved in it.

I recently received a phone call in my office and, upon looking at my Caller ID, saw the call letters of a local television station pop up. (Rule number one for any consultant: you are never too busy to talk to a reporter.) I answered the phone, and the reporter introduced herself and said, "Mike Murphy told me that you are the hiring guru and that I should talk to you." Mike, a contact from church, knew both what I do and what help he could give me because we were involved together in our community. Instead of being just another handshake on Sunday mornings, Mike has become a friend and an important member of my network. The conversation with the reporter culminated in my taping an interview that aired on the evening news.

What's my point? Despite the fact that my fellow churchgoers are not a particularly high-profile group, there are members with valuable connections. In terms of building your network, it's better to be a highly committed leader in a smaller group than a hanger-on in a large one. Leaders get respect. Don't get me wrong; if you had to choose between hanging out with a group of chief executives or a group of temporary workers, you would take the CEOs. But in the end, if you just hang around the fringes of the CEO group, you will never get any traction. Pick a group that you care about and get deeply involved. You will be pleasantly surprised at the connections you can make.

> **A-Player Principle:** Don't wallow in the shallow end of business and community groups. Pick one or two, and dive deep. The relationships you build working side by side with other like-minded people will pay off in A-player contacts.

Quality Is More Important than Quantity

While any group has influential members who can help you to find A-players, not all groups are created equally. I once spoke to an audience of only seven business owners and got three new clients out of it. Ever since that happened, I focus less on the size of such groups and more on the quality and influence of the people in them. A smaller group of decision makers is typically more valuable to you than a big group of middle managers (unless you are building a farm team of A-player middle managers).

When Lyndon Johnson was a member of the U.S. House of Representatives, he loathed every minute of it. It was too big—435 members—and he struggled to have any influence as a junior congressman. However, when Johnson was elected to the U.S. Senate, he stood in the Senate chamber, observed the much smaller group of 100 senators at work, and said to himself, "It's just the right size."[1] He knew that in this smaller but more influential group, he could wield real power.

If you find that this quality versus quantity approach works for you too, join a group that is filled with decision makers, invest in it, and help it to grow and develop. In the process, you will build relationships that will help to fill your farm team and provide the next generation of A-players for your organization.

> **A-Player Principle:** It's not the size of the group that matters; it's the quality of the people in it. Typically, an investment of time with a small group of decision makers is worth more than one with a large group of middle managers.

Develop Connections to Influencers

Influencers are well-respected leaders to whom others look for guidance. These people are often in roles that help them to know and be known by a large group of people. Business owners, volunteer and paid business association leaders, university professors, chamber of commerce board members, school principals, religious leaders, and the head of your child's parent teacher organization often fit this description. The list goes on and on. The key is this: determine which individuals are the Influencers in your world and cultivate your relationships with them.

To start, develop relationships with influential people who share your interests. Let's say that you love to ride Harleys. Then the owner of the local Harley dealership is a natural Influencer in that arena. He or she is connected to a huge number of people who share your passion and is the go-to person when this group is looking for advice. Perhaps you have kids involved with athletics. Your child's coach may be a natural Influencer for that group of people. He knows every kid on the team and every parent of every kid. Reach out to such people and tell them that you are always looking for talented people for your team. Be intentional about cultivating relationships with influential people in the spheres in which you move. Here are some more examples of Influencers with whom you can cultivate relationships.

Recruiters from Other Companies

Internal recruiters who work for other companies can be Influencers and terrific sources for A-player referrals. For example, Northwestern Mutual Financial Network (as well as many other insurance companies) has a well-developed recruiting system. It takes every candidate through a series of interviews and online assessments. If candidates fail to pass any of these steps, they don't advance to the next level of interviews. However, if your A-player profile does not require the same hard-core sales skills that these companies are looking for, candidates who don't fit their needs could be a great fit for you. So look for industries and companies that have well-developed recruiting machines. Figure out who oversees recruiting for the local offices of these companies and strike up a relationship. Refer people to them, encourage referrals to you, and see if you can uncover a few more A-players in the process.

> **A-Player Principle:** Find insurance executives, real estate executives, or other businesspeople who recruit all the time. Learn their A-player profile, educate them about yours, and see if you can help one another to find more A-players.

Office Managers

Tom McKendry is a terrific salesperson and tailor for Tom James, the world's largest manufacturer and retailer of custom clothing. McKendry is in and out of corporate offices all day long, and he becomes well acquainted with a lot of office managers in the process. He knows that these people interact with salespeople like him all day long and are Influencers in their realms. So Tom lets them know that if they refer a salesperson whom he hires, they will get

$1,000 of Tom James clothing as a referral gift. You know that every office supply, bottled water, and copier salesperson is getting the once-over from Tom's office manager friends. They want those clothes!

Rewards like these are not bribes. They are simply a "thank you" that keeps your A-player profile top of mind for people in your network. If people take the time to help you hire an A-player, why wouldn't you reward them for doing so?

> **A-Player Principle:** Offer recruiting referral gifts as a well-earned thank you. People are busy. If someone takes the time to refer an A-player to you, provide him or her with a tangible token of your appreciation. It will make that person more likely to refer to you again.

Take Your Time

When you're developing relationships with Influencers, don't start off by immediately trying to tap into their A-player network. These people are targeted by everyone, so their defenses are up. Instead, get to know them. Ask questions and listen, don't just talk and tell. Over time, educate them about your business and your A-player Profile. Let them know that you constantly interview. Sooner or later, this will pay off in referrals from highly credible sources.

Only good things happen when you develop relationships with Influencers. These people can be terrific sources of A-player referrals. They can also help you to acquire new clients, establish a higher profile in your business community, meet other influential movers and shakers, and gain access to schools, clubs, and networks that you would never reach on your own.

Follow Through

If you want to kill your ability to generate A-player referrals, simply fail to follow through on the referrals that you do receive. When

Influencers—or anyone else—refer potential employees to you, *make sure* to:

1. Phone screen or interview people promptly.
2. Help them to meet other decision makers if you decide not to hire them.
3. Follow up with your referral sources no matter the outcome. Thank them for their help and keep them in the loop regarding the interview process.

> **A-Player Principle:** Influencers are critical referral sources. Write down the names of three to five of these people. How can you develop relationships with them so that you can ultimately generate A-player referrals?

Become an Influencer Yourself

One of the best ways to find more A-players is to become an Influencer yourself. Raise your own profile and meet more influential people in the process. There are many great ways to do this. Here are two great real-life examples.

Join a Board

A friend of mine served on a Junior Achievement board with the president of a local bank. Upon learning that my friend ran a recruiting organization, the bank president leaned over to him at a meeting and said, "Young man, there is a problem that I am running into in our organization. Is this something you can help me with?" One million dollars later, my friend's genuine commitment to Junior Achievement had also significantly paid off for his business. Get involved in groups and increase your own influence—your access to influential people will naturally increase.

Become an Adjunct Professor

Many colleges and universities offer professionals the opportunity to serve as adjunct professors. Not only do these roles enhance your credibility, they put you in touch with a big pool of potential A-players.

Todd Gibson is chief executive officer of Gibson Media, a Seattle-based advertising agency. Every morning during the school year, Todd teaches a communication class at Highline Community College. Teaching this class is a great way for him to give back to the community and a smart way to identify entry-level A-players. Todd gets to see students in action over a three-month academic quarter and discerns which ones are highly effective. After grades are in and the quarter ends, he often offers internships to the best of these students, which in turn can lead to full-time jobs. As Todd says, "Teaching keeps me engaged with cutting-edge material and helps me to stay in tune with the issues, passions, and concerns of younger people. It also gives me a built-in opportunity to screen students as potential interns and employees."

Todd's class includes live-fire assignments that get students interacting with executives in the local business community. For example, every quarter he asks each student to report on a Seattle area business that is giving back to the community. The students have to identify and contact the businesses, set up interviews with the executives, and conduct the interviews at the companies' offices. They then deliver a six- to eight-minute presentation to the class reviewing what they learned. The assignment challenges students to use and develop skills that really matter in business. It also reveals which class members are proactive, organized, and effective communicators.

Todd always waits until a class is completed and grades have been submitted before offering students an internship, as it's generally not a good idea to have a conversation about employment with a current student. However, after they've completed his class, Todd often approaches the top one or two students about an opportunity at his company. Gibson Media structures its internships to last from one to three academic quarters and pays at least $15 per hour (which is better than most student jobs). Students can also earn academic credit at the rate of 1 credit hour for every 30 hours worked.

Teaching helps to make Todd an Influencer. It gives him a perfect opportunity to see a lot of sharp people in action and to determine over time who has the potential to be an A-player in his business and industry. As Todd says, "During job interviews, we all tend to make snap judgments and then justify our first reactions. In my situation, I develop my impression of the person over three months. It is a much more logical and effective way to evaluate people."

Cultivating Referral Sources

When it comes to cultivating referral sources for A-players, keep in mind that maintaining these relationships does not have to take a lot of time if you do it right. Here are five steps to follow.

1. **Connect.** Get introduced to people. Ask questions and be a good listener. Figure out how you can be of value to others so they will want to be of value to you.
2. **Educate.** Educate people about your A-Player Profile. Often others will have misperceptions about the talents you seek. The Tom James Company, for instance, looks for great salespeople whom they can train to be great tailors, not the other way around. Take the time to educate people about the talents you really want.
3. **Refer.** The best way to get people to help you is to help *them*. Look for any opportunity to refer potential employees, potential clients, or just good contacts to these referrals sources.
4. **Remind.** You have to remind people that you are around so that they remember to help you. Use e-mail reminders, quick phone calls, LinkedIn, Twitter, or any other tool you can to alert people about you and your company. Remind them that you are always interviewing and on the lookout for A-players.
5. **Put it on autopilot.** It does not take much time to maintain these relationships if you are staying in touch electronically. Some of these referral connections will be productive over time, while some will not. If you get just one or two A-player referrals from a source over the course of a year, your time has been well invested.

Do I Really Have Time for This?

The steps that I describe in this chapter are critical not just for finding A-players but also for finding new clients, developing your career, and building your business. I am not asking you to do a lot more than you already are doing when it comes to getting out in the community and building new business relationships. Instead, I am giving you some strategies to make the networking that you are already doing *pay off* in finding and hiring A-players. Every day you meet people who could help you find your next great employee. You rob yourself and your business of crucial opportunities if you don't have a step-by-step process for cultivating these relationships and tapping into them for A-players.

A search consultant told me a great story about the importance of patiently cultivating relationships. A CEO asked her to find an A-player to fill a senior executive role. She found the perfect guy—and he turned her down cold. This executive was content with his current company. However, this recruiter wouldn't quit. It took her nine months to convince this man just to have breakfast with her client. No commitments, just breakfast. Three months after the breakfast finally occurred, this same executive quit his job and went to work for her client. The breakfast meeting was the first step in his realizing that this would be a great career move. This and subsequent meetings convinced him that he and the CEO could work as partners to achieve a common vision. Just as important, this executive connected with the CEO relationally. He realized that this was someone he could work with, learn from, and follow.

Strong performers want leaders they can follow and who have a vision they can buy into. When you expand your network, you are increasing the number of A-players you know who share your values and passion. Some of these people will buy into your leadership and vision; they are the future A-players of your company. But if you just sit in your office or hang out with the same small circle of people, you will never find these people. So get focused, be purposeful about expanding your network, and start filling your farm team with new talent.

A-Player Payoff Points

Chapter 5: Don't Just Sit There. Reach Out!

- Be the recruiter in chief for your business by getting everyone to focus on finding A-players.
- Find fertile A-player hunting grounds, such as continuing education classes and industry conferences. Intentionally cultivate relationships at these events. Some of your competitors are probably already doing so.
- Invest your time in at least one business or community group. Develop connections as you demonstrate your leadership.
- Identify Influencers to add leverage to your recruiting efforts.
- Become an Influencer yourself. Expand your personal brand and access to A-players.
- Be patient and foster relationships both with A-players and Influencers. Just one new A-player can make all the time and effort pay off.

6

Finding New Pools of A-Player Talent

People who grew up on family farms. Junior military officers. College athletes. What do all three of these groups have in common? These are just a few of the specific talent pools from which executives love to find A-players. And here's why.

People who grew up on farms have worked hard all their lives. They woke up early every day to get things done on the farm before they went to school. They understand just how hard you have to work to keep a business running. They already have the work ethic that is so important for success.

Junior military officers know what it means to lead people and have had to assume a lot of responsibility at an early age. Structured, hierarchical organizations feel like a good fit to them. JMOs bring these abilities with them to their new careers.

College athletes essentially work two jobs through college (school and sports). They are competitive, committed, and willing to do what it takes to achieve their goals. Plenty of executives—particularly those who share this background—place a premium on these abilities and love to hire former college athletes.

Do the skills above line up well with your company's A-player profile? If they do, you can focus your recruiting efforts on one or more of these talent pools. As you know, there are skills that you can teach (technical knowledge, product knowledge, understanding of a particular client) and skills you can't (motivation, leadership, commitment, the ability to sell, and the desire to achieve). Once you know your A-player profile, it only makes sense to find a pool of people who already possess the hard-to-teach skills that are vital to your company. Once you find such a pool, you need to interview a lot of people in order to consistently find A-players. Then hire the best people you find and teach them what they need to know to be A-players in your business.

This chapter is filled with additional examples of specific talent pools for finding A-players. Remember, finding just one great pool of talent for your business can dramatically improve your hiring results.

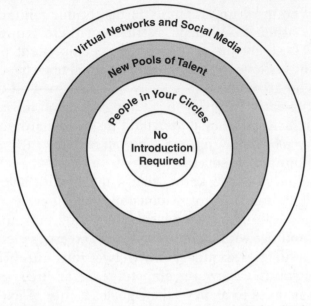

FIGURE 6.1   Sources of A-Players: New Pools of Talent

A-Player Principle: There are skills you can teach and skills you can't. Find a large pool of people who already have the fundamental skills you want, interview a lot of them, and hire the best of them. This is a simple formula for creating a team of A-players.

Women Reentering the Workforce

If you can offer flexible hours at your company, you may be able to hire from one of the best pools of talent available today: well-educated women with professional experience who are reentering the workforce or reconfiguring their careers after having children. While more men are staying home with children, this talent pool is still overwhelmingly made up of women. In 2008, the United States had approximately 5.5 million stay-at-home parents, comprised of 5.3 million mothers and 140,000 fathers.[1]

Our world is full of smart, accomplished women who want to have a balance in their lives between raising a family and being engaged in the workplace. People become extremely stressed when they try to pull off having careers, raising kids, and still having some semblance of a personal life. If you can provide job candidates the kind of flexibility that allows them to do interesting work and still handle their responsibilities at home, you will have a valuable offering that will appeal to some very sharp people. Companies all over the world use various strategies to tap into these underutilized employees. The key is to hone in on a specific slice of this huge talent pool, determine how to make contact, and then interview a constant stream of these people. Here are three successful examples.

Spouses of Relocated Executives

I work with an incentive travel company in Houston that has had ongoing success hiring A-player women who have moved to the area for their husbands' careers in the energy industry. The president of the hiring company has made a concerted effort to cultivate contacts in the industry, specifically with the individuals who handle relocations for these large corporations. These people serve as resources for the families moving in and can offer information about which companies to contact for quality jobs with flexible hours. My client now has a reputation as a great source for this kind of employment. These women have strong resumes but don't want to work full time in the midst of a stressful and time-consuming relocation process. They are smart, effective, get a lot done working part-time hours, and are therefore a perfect fit for this company.

Single-Mother Waitresses

To fill its sales positions, Doorway Rug (mentioned in Chapter 2) hired A-players out of the restaurant industry, many of whom were working mothers. The demands of simultaneously raising children and working nights and weekends were very difficult. Doorway Rug targeted these women with its recruiting efforts, offered them a salary equivalent to their restaurant position, but provided flexible hours. The flexibility was worth more than a dollar or two more per hour to these women, and the company was able to hire some terrific people using this approach.

Big-Firm Lawyers Who Don't Want Big-Firm Hours

I work with a local law firm that has done a great job of building an A-player team with women who are reentering the workforce. This firm, made up of about 10 attorneys plus support people, has created a part-time, flexible work arrangement for some of its attorneys. The program has attracted several women who graduated from elite law schools, worked for big-time firms, and then took time off to have kids. They wanted to get back into law but knew that the hours they used to work at their old firms would not fit into their current lives. They are now very happy working for this small firm, which in turn has built a staff with credentials that rival those of vastly bigger operations.

The A-player women who work for these companies want the same things most people want: challenging work, fair pay, and reasonable hours. For many people, time is worth more than money. If you can create flexible hours and work arrangements in your company, you will be able to hire talent that you may have thought was unattainable. It's not easy for A-players to find great full-time roles, much less a company for which they can do meaningful work and have flexible or part-time hours. If you offer significant work, competitive pay, and flexibility, you have a very strong value proposition for an A-player. What are the specific slices of this fantastic talent pool that would provide the best potential employees for you? Identify whom you want to recruit, then get out there and promote your opportunities to the best people you know.

A-Player Principle: There is a large pool of talented women who want to keep a hand in their profession but don't want to work full time. This may be one of the best pools of underutilized A-player talent available today. Consider how to structure a role that attracts this kind of employee.

How Do You Find Them?

Where do you go to find these A-player women who want to reenter the workforce? Here are some ideas.

- Tap into the university and corporate alumni networks. People who are reentering the workforce often reach out to their former organizations to make contacts.
- Contact anyone and everyone you know in your own industry, and educate them about the accommodating role that you are providing. If you are a local CPA firm, for instance, and you are offering a flexible staff accounting role, call people you know at the Big Four firms and ask them for referrals. You may get a shot at hiring people to whom you never would have had access for a traditional full-time role.
- Use a public relations person to secure interviews on local television stations or in your regional newspaper regarding the flexible work options you provide. This is a compelling issue for reporters. If you are successful in getting featured in the media, the exposure will help you to broaden your network.
- Create an ongoing buzz in your LinkedIn, Facebook, and Twitter entries about looking for great people who are interested in flexible hours. You will reach people who would be impossible to connect with any other way.
- Speak to industry groups and business associations about how you use flexible work arrangements to build an A-player culture. This is a hot topic. If you are a half-decent speaker, you won't have any problems finding an audience. Your talk becomes an opportunity to provide value and promote your company to A-players. Trust me; people will approach you after your program to talk about employment.
- Educate your Influencers (discussed in Chapter 5) about the flexible role you are providing. This is exactly the kind of win-win situation that will make them want to tap into their personal and professional networks to help you find the right person.

Restaurant Personnel

Have you ever worked in a restaurant? The dining room is clean and inviting. Depending on how upscale a restaurant is, it may be beautiful, serene, or funky. But it is always a stage on which a performance is played out during breakfast, lunch, and dinner. The kitchen, however, is another story. It is hot, crowded, loud, and profane. Miraculously, out of this maelstrom emerges beautifully prepared food that is presented with a flourish to diners who have no idea of the drama that unfolded to make their plate so appealing.

Between these two worlds are the waitstaff who must build immediate rapport with customers, know their products intimately, make good recommendations, and up-sell with expertly delivered phrases. While you probably don't operate a restaurant, the requirements of this job likely sound familiar. Every business has to make its product or service and deliver it flawlessly to clients. Bridging the gap between the kitchen and the dining room are the salespeople who create enthusiastic customers who want to come back again and again.

Steve Schultz is a successful sales manager in the copier and document imaging industry. He will tell you that people who have excelled as waiters, waitresses, or restaurant managers often do well for him in entry-level sales positions. Steve likes hiring A-players from the restaurant industry because they:

- Are service-oriented.
- Are transactional—they deal with customers all the time and make quick sales.
- Understand the importance of solving customer problems immediately.
- Know how to up-sell.
- Are used to customers making quick judgments on the quality of their service.
- Understand their pay (tip) is a scorecard for the service they have delivered.

When you look at it this way, the best waiters and waitresses could be a great fit for a lot of businesses.

How Do You Find Them?

If it sounds like many of these characteristics fit your A-player profile, then you'll want to figure out how to connect with them. Here are some specific steps you can take.

- Get intentional about developing your network with these people. Who do you know right now who works in the restaurant industry, or who knows someone who does? Reach out to them, and educate them about the opportunities at your company.
- When you get business cards or contact information from people in the restaurant industry, enter them in your contact database and make a note of their type of business. Down the road, send a targeted e-mail to all your restaurant contacts with a job posting designed to appeal to them.
- Connect with these people through social media tools like LinkedIn, Facebook, and Twitter. Keep your social media network updated on your company's growth and the ongoing career opportunities for A-players. Your contacts will pass these postings along and help you to find more restaurant personnel.
- Highlight the advantages your company offers over a restaurant job: regular hours, flexible hours, better pay, better benefits, and a strong career path.
- Turn every lunch and dinner that you eat in a restaurant into a recruiting session. Strike up a conversation with every great waiter, waitress, and restaurant manager you meet. Give them your card, have them check your company's web site, and ask if you can enroll them for your corporate newsletter to keep them updated on career opportunities.
- Make sure that your web site features a career section that promotes positions at your company in an appealing way.

- Run employment ads that emphasize the advantages of your role in the restaurant section of job boards such as craigslist .org, Monster.com, and CareerBuilder.com.

Teachers

For years, life insurance companies and stock brokerage firms have had special programs set up specifically to recruit teachers. A senior executive in the brokerage industry told me that he loves to hire teachers because they are great communicators, know a lot of people, have strong interpersonal skills, and are vastly underpaid. His company enrolled teachers in special programs that allowed them to begin their financial services careers during the summers while teaching during the school year. Without fail, some got a taste of financial success and moved into a full-time financial service career.

Beyond the financial services industry, I know companies involved in everything from home remodeling to retail that have successfully turned teachers into A-player employees. The key is to create a program in which teachers work full time during the summers when they are not teaching and then have a scaled-down schedule during the school year. They get a feel for your business during this program, and you get a feel for their drive and abilities. Over the course of a couple of summers, you discover which individuals could be full-time A-players for your business.

We, of course, need A-player teachers. But not every sharp person who begins a career in the classroom will stay for the duration. Some of those who leave could be great for your team. If you think former teachers fit your A-player profile, establish a program that gets them on your farm team and working in your business.

How Do You Find Them?

Start asking around your community for contacts in the world of teaching. Many teachers are looking for additional ways to make money. If your program for them is strong, you should have no trouble coming up with contacts. Consider running a "Teachers' Night" where you introduce them to the opportunities at your business. If you are successful at tapping into this network, people will refer their friends, and you will begin filling your recruiting pipeline with educators who could turn into your next A-players.

Starbucks and Other Well-Operated National Retailers

Your next A-player may well be the guy who makes your latte every morning at Starbucks. Companies like Starbucks have very well-developed hiring and training systems. They offer relatively strong benefits, which helps them to attract good people. You, in turn, get to see their employees in action on every visit and observe how they handle the demands of serving multiple customers simultaneously. Over time, you can build relationships here that turn into great hires.

Realize that you are on a recruiting trip every time you visit *any business establishment*. Pay attention to the receptionist, the secretaries, the staff, the managers, and the executives; any one of them could be your next hire. When you spot people doing a great job, strike up conversations. Learn their names. Tell them how well they are doing—and leave it at that. On subsequent visits, carry on the conversation and continue to build rapport. You can say to them at some point—perhaps a few weeks down the road: "My company is growing, and we are hiring some more people. Do you know anyone who would be interested in a position doing X?" This is also a natural time to give them your business card. Your approach is soft, not pushy; friendly, not creepy.

You might not get much of a response the first time you take this approach. However, you have planted a seed. Over the course of the coming weeks and months, if you plant enough seeds with enough good people, something will grow.

Clients of mine who run a franchise frequented their neighborhood Starbucks and were impressed with a young man who worked behind the counter. They followed the steps just described and found out that they all had some common friends and interests. After that, when my clients visited the store, this Starbucks employee greeted them like old friends. Several months later, he interviewed with them for a job. He wanted to work for them and my clients wanted to hire him, but in a strange twist of events, he moved cities and subsequently went to work for a different franchise in the same chain. Today this man is a true A-player for this second franchise. He has strong leadership as well as sales skills. He is already playing a management role just a few months after taking the job. All because my clients paid attention to their barista.

How Do You Find Them?

- Remember that every visit you make to every business establishment is a recruiting trip.
- Pay attention to the people you meet at other businesses. Who is performing like an A-player?
- Take the time to tell strong performers that they are doing a great job. Introduce yourself and strike up a conversation.
- Build rapport, but be low-key about it. Eventually you can tell high performers that your company is hiring and ask them if they know anyone. If people are interested, they will let you know. Don't forget to give them your card.
- Don't be concerned if this immediate invitation does not result in a new hire. The goal is to build connections with people and cast seeds. If you do that enough, it will result in strong hires.

> **A-Player Principle:** Life is an interview. Watch for A-players in every interaction that you have and find ways to begin relationships and to stay in touch. You will find some great people for your farm team this way.

On-Campus Interviewing

An increasing number of companies in professional services and other fields know that they have to develop their own talent in order to stay competitive. Milhouse & Neal, just such a company, is a leading local CPA firm in St. Louis. This firm, like many others, has difficulty hiring experienced senior accountants, particularly when the economy is strong. It decided that part of the solution was to develop its own talent. (Recall the importance of incubating your own talent, discussed in Chapter 3). One step it took to recruit A-players was to build strong relationships with several of the local universities.

Shirley Ann Rizi oversees marketing for the firm and took on some of the recruiting responsibilities as well (another great example of leveraging your current marketing resources to find A-players). Shirley Ann decided to establish connections with colleges in the area that had strong accounting departments. She went beyond just introducing herself to the career placement offices. She cultivated relationships directly with key professors in these accounting programs. She let them know that the A-Player Profile at Milhouse & Neal calls for strong leadership qualities as well as strong accounting skills, and she requested their help in referring their best students. The professors believed in Shirley Ann and understood what she was looking for in a new hire. As a result, they started referring some of their top student leaders to her firm.

> **A-Player Principle:** On-campus recruiting is not just for the Fortune 500. Develop relationships with on-campus Influencers who can refer students that fit your A-player profile.

Students and Irregular Hours

Keep in mind that if your company offers irregular hours (evenings or weekends), there are dependable students who may be interested in working for you. Whether they are undergraduates or graduate students, there are young people out there who are looking for positions with hours that fit their school schedules. I know several businesses that successfully employ students for several years while they finish their degrees. Are there specific university programs that fit well with your business? If so, introduce your company to the directors of the program and create associations at the school. Jobs you typically find difficult to fill may be perfect for this group.

Internships

One great way to expand your farm team and develop connections with A-players is to create an internship program. Michael Vaughan is vice president of sales for TicketLeap, a start-up company that allows event organizers to sell tickets online. Mike and others at the company have strong connections with the Wharton Business School and other schools within the University of Pennsylvania. They used these connections to develop an internship program through which they hire a significant percentage of their full-time employees. When the company had only 22 employees, 5 or 6 of them were college interns, and another 3 or 4 of the full-timers had started out as interns.

Here are Mike's pointers on tapping into universities using internships to find and hire A-players:

- College students are trained to be researchers. Any job that you can structure to be research oriented is a great fit for a college student with intelligence and a strong work ethic.
- When you hire students, you also tap into their network of relationships. By creating a good internship program, you create positive word of mouth that helps you to attract next year's interns.
- The company's executives must stay in touch with their university contacts to make these programs really work. These relationships help to increase your internship program's visibility at the school and help you to tap into other university-related contacts who would be good employees.

Internships fit into a farm team recruiting strategy because you are essentially trying people out before you hire them. It won't take more than a month or two for you to figure out who are the best-performing interns. Even if you keep a talented intern for only one summer, your company is typically better off for having hired an A-player. Some students can continue to work as interns during the school year, while others will become full-time employees after graduation. Furthermore, if your internship program is strong, this year's interns will spread the word to younger students that your program is worthwhile. This helps you to fill next year's program with potential A-players.

Even One Intern Can Make a Difference

Gazelles Inc. (www.gazelles.com) offers leadership development and executive coaching to fast-growth businesses. Chief executive Verne Harnish recently hired an especially intelligent high school student as a summer intern with a specific focus on improving the company's social media presence. This teenager already had 20,000 people following him personally on Twitter, so why not have him improve Gazelles' profile there, on Facebook, and other online social media outlets? As Verne says, "I rescued him from Smoothie King, which is where he was going to work in order to earn enough money to get a high-end laptop to drive his own business venture." As compensation for his internship with Gazelles, the intern got the laptop he wanted along with a much more valuable summer job experience than working at Smoothie King. Verne and Gazelles got the improved social media presence for which they were looking. Furthermore, Gazelles now has one more A-player on its farm team. Here are some additional lessons that can be gleaned from Verne's approach:

- **Have a plan.** Particularly during the first week, Verne gave this young man a number of books to read on social media. While Verne liked his knowledge and ambition, he didn't just leave him to his own devices. He did everything he could to make sure the internship was a success.
- **Define the program's goals.** Like every other position out there, you have to define the focus of an internship in order to get the best results from it. I like Verne's approach—he focused

on specific, measurable deliverables (e.g., "Gazelles will have a company Facebook page up by the end of the summer"). This helps to ensure that your business gets real value from this investment of time and that your intern has a great experience.

- **Get them engaged.** Take your interns along on meetings. Include them in events. Get them involved with your clients in appropriate ways. This kind of contact makes an internship particularly valuable. Such involvement in turn encourages your interns to tell their friends about your program and helps you to recruit more A-player students for next year's program.
- **Compensate reasonably, but don't overpay.** Verne hired a bright student, compensated him fairly, and gave him invaluable experience. The best intern is someone who values the experience you are providing as much as the money you are paying.

A-Player Principle: Just one intern can make a difference—you don't need 10 students in such a program to have an impact. If you are serious about creating a team of A-players, adding an internship program is one of the ways you can do it.

Alumni Networks of Large Companies

IBM, Ernst & Young, KPMG, Accenture—name any large company, and chances are that it has a well-developed alumni network. These firms know that only a small percentage of their employees stay for their whole careers. The majority of their employees ultimately leave, and it is important to these companies to maintain strong relationships with them. After all, the alumni often turn into clients.

If you or your employees used to work for such companies, an immediate action item for you is to get more involved with these alumni networks. Most of these organizations have an online presence for their alumni where you can register and search for others. Retained search professionals will tell you that this is one of their favorite hunting grounds for building relationships with high-quality people. You will find that leveraging past relationships—particularly those built in your school and early career years—will pay significant dividends in A-player contacts and referrals.

Former Entrepreneurs

Often you will hear executives say that they don't hire entrepreneurs as employees because as soon as they get back on their feet, they will leave to start their next venture. However, some former entrepreneurs love being free of the burdens and responsibilities of small business ownership.

Vita Burdi of DJ's Home Improvements, a kitchen and bath remodeler in Franklin Square, New York, finds that people who have run their own carpentry businesses are terrific for overseeing her carpentry crews. They are seasoned professionals who managed companies on their own for 10 years or more but are tired of the headaches of owning a business and are ready to have someone else worry about making payroll. These individuals know what it means to be committed to customer service. They understand the people side *and* the carpentry side of the business, plus they make sure their crews do great work and get things done on time.

How Do You Find Them?

Consider the type of former small-business owners who could be a great fit for your team. If you are a kitchen and bath company like DJ's and you want to hire the former owners of carpentry firms, your recruiting takes place every day that you conduct your business. Develop relationships with a wide range of carpenters. Find the people who do the best job and recruit the A-players. If you own an advertising firm, you may want to hire a full-time account manager from among the freelancers with whom you work. This is another situation where you can hire people on a project basis, put them on your farm team, and actively recruit the A-players. This same approach works for turning consultants, CPAs, attorneys, and other professional service providers into A-player employees. Every project they complete is part of the interview process.

> **A-Player Principle:** Don't always accept common wisdom. For certain roles, employing people who have run their own businesses is a good strategy. They have great organizational skills—but some people never want to deal with the headaches of business ownership again.

Find a Talent Pool and Go Deep

You need to tap into only one of these talent pools to make a big difference for your company. Experiment with different industries and backgrounds to find a group of people who make sense for your farm team. Once you find the right one, go deep: Develop as many relationships as you can. If you tap into a particular set of people—all of whom have the basic skills and experiences that you want—and then you interview a lot of these people, you will find some A-players. The key is to find as many people as possible who fit your A-player profile, then use your interviewing process to separate the wheat from the chaff.

A-Player Payoff Points

Chapter 6: Finding New Pools of A-Player Talent

- Look for highly skilled women who are reentering the workforce after raising children. If you can, offer them the flexibility they want. They can be terrific talent for your company.

- Many transactional sales organizations find that former waiters and waitresses do well in their business model. Expand your network in this talent pool and hire the most exceptional people you find.
- Teachers have strong people skills and excellent communication abilities, and often are underpaid. Look for ways to utilize them during the summer months and provide them with flexibility during the school year. Some of them may become full-time A-players.
- Starbucks and other national retailers offer a pool of well-trained staff. Every time you interact with employees at these stores, you are interviewing them. Establish connections with those who most impress you, and over time, you may bring some of them into your own organization.
- Even small companies can succeed at attracting top talent on campus. Build relationships with professors and other Influencers who can help you to connect with the students who fit your A-Player Profile.
- Design an internship program at your company to cultivate A-player talent. Set clear goals for the program and create a great experience that generates positive word of mouth and quality referrals for the following year's program.

7

The Basics of Online Recruiting

I recently participated in a webinar that explained the business uses of social media tools such as LinkedIn, Facebook, and Twitter. The firm that conducted the training, based in San Francisco, does nothing but consult on Internet-based marketing and sales. Though the two session leaders were social media "experts," both said that as of 18 months earlier, neither of them knew much about Twitter. A year and a half later, they were talking about it being the next great Internet marketing tool. If high-tech consultants who had barely heard of Twitter a year and a half ago are now the go-to experts, the rest of us can be excused for being slightly overwhelmed by the hype that surrounds these tools.

We live in a time of extraordinary and rapid technological change. As business leaders, we have to make adjustments to keep in step. I was listening to a radio station in my car the other day that was advertising its latest listener promotion—the kind that requires you to be listening at 2 a.m. and be the twenty-seventh caller to win an all-inclusive trip for two to the Caribbean. At the tail end of the advertisement came the usual legal disclaimer spoken in hushed tones and at extraordinary speed. The announcer spoke so quickly that I almost missed a piece of legalese I had never heard before. The deep radio voice said: "Only listeners in the terrestrial listening area of this station are eligible to win this promotion." I assume this means that if you live in Brisbane, Australia, and listen to this Philadelphia station via streaming audio over the Web, you are not eligible to win. We have gotten to the point where a phrase like "terrestrial listening area"—which sounds like something out of science fiction—is *required* due to the technology that gives even local radio stations global reach.

The good news is that this same new technology enhances your ability to create an A-player team. In addition to the online job boards (which have been around a long time), LinkedIn, Facebook, Twitter, and similar tools enable your company to expand the breadth and depth of your recruiting reach dramatically with limited additional cost.

These tools are important to recruiting. The question is: how can busy executives use them most effectively to find and hire A-players? I lay out the basics of online recruiting in this chapter. If

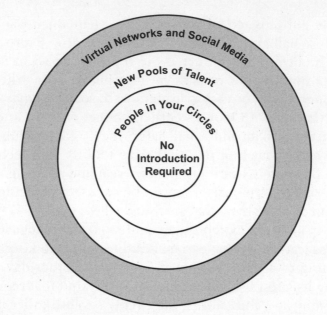

FIGURE 7.1 Sources of A-Players: Virtual Networks and Social Media

you have a dedicated recruiting department, you have surely already engaged in these activities. Use the material presented here to improve your online recruiting efforts. If you don't have a recruiting department, this material can serve as a game plan for incorporating these tools into your strategy for creating an A-player team.

Your Company's Web Site

Your web site—one of your company's critical marketing tools—is also vital for recruiting. The first thing that most job seekers do to learn about your company is check you out on the Web. They want to see the same things that your clients and prospects want to see: a professionally created site that provides a strong overview of what you do and who makes up your company.

Employment Web Page

You should have an employment section on your web site that reflects your commitment to building a team of A-players. No matter the day or time, it should be clear to me when I look at your web site that your company is *always* interested in finding the next A-player.

There is virtually no limit to the technology you can employ to turn your web site into a recruiting center. However, many of my clients want to know the *minimum* amount of time and money they can invest and still have their web sites be effective recruiting tools. At the very least, your site's employment section should:

- Create a consistent, positive impression of your company and brand.
- Communicate your A-player profile so that candidates can begin to decide if they are a fit for you.
- Make it easy for candidates to apply for a job with your company.
- Allow you to respond quickly to the people who apply.

A-Player Principle: You don't have to spend a lot of money to transform your web site into an effective A-player recruiting tool. Make sure that it gives potential employees the content they want when they want it and that it makes it easy to apply for a job.

A Great Example

Figure 7.2 shows an example of a simple, professional, and to-the-point employment page on a company web site. My clients Dink and Suzanne Taylor, owners of the Fleet Feet Sports franchise in Huntsville, Alabama, are committed to hiring A-players and they know their A-Player Profile. Check out the employment page on their company's web site (www.fleetfeethuntsville.com/employment-0). This is where you'll see the company's A-player profile described in a conversational format that helps people decide for themselves if this company is right for them. Dink and Suzanne

FIGURE 7.2   Fleet Feet Sports Huntsville Employment Web Page

will be the first to tell you that they learned and borrowed from fellow business owners in coming up with their site. But they have done a good job of pulling it all together and gave me permission to share their work with you.

I've described the A-Player Profile from the Taylors' web site in bullet-point form next. The actual employment page includes a one-paragraph description for each A-player criterion:

Are you right for Fleet Feet Huntsville? Is Fleet Feet Huntsville right for you? Test yourself with these questions:

- Do you have a sales sense?
- Are you good at switching gears?
- Can you stay calm and friendly under pressure?
- Are you a team player?
- Are you willing to learn new things?
- Do you pay attention to the little things?
- Are you patient and willing to serve people?
- Are you available on weekends?

I like this page because it speaks directly to the person who is considering applying and communicates exactly what the company is looking for. You can tell from the first three questions that this is a company that knows what it wants from an employee. The best applicants will speak directly to these criteria during their interview, explain why they are excited about the job, and give examples of how they can sell, switch gears, and stay calm and friendly under pressure.

Simple Works

While the Taylors' page is professionally done, it is also the height of simplicity. Job applicants send an e-mail directly to the store manager by clicking on the "e-mail us" link. There are very powerful applicant-tracking systems on the market that automatically accept online applications and allow you to keep track of your potential employees. If you are to the point in your business where that kind of system makes sense, then by all means pursue it. However, you don't have to have these sophisticated systems in order to leverage the Web to create an A-player team.

Remember Your Knockout Factors

Communicate your knockout factors clearly when you create the employment page for your web site. This encourages people to screen themselves out of contention and helps you to eliminate unqualified candidates early in the interview process. Fleet Feet Huntsville's employment page asks about work availability because working nights and weekends is critical to this role. When you download the employment application, you'll find that it also has a section that asks applicants to specify the number of hours they can work. In most cases, people with very limited availability to work are eliminated from consideration.

> **A-Player Principle:** Include a version of your A-Player Profile in the employment section of your web site and be explicit about your knockout factors. This helps poorly qualified people to eliminate themselves from consideration and helps you to weed out weak candidates quickly.

Following Up on Employment Applications

If people apply online to your business, at a minimum they should receive:

1. An e-mail acknowledging the application and indicating that your company will follow up with them. If you create a dedicated e-mail box for employment applications, turn the auto

responder on to send this acknowledgment immediately. Give people a time frame (5 to 10 days) in which your company will respond to the application.

2. A polite rejection letter/e-mail to every applicant you choose not to pursue. You can never have too many friends. There is no reason to create bad rapport by not acknowledging an employment application.

3. A follow-up e-mail and/or phone call to every applicant with whom you are interested in speaking directly.

Make It Easy on Yourself

Do yourself a favor: Delegate to others the responsibility for following up on employment applications and for scheduling—and even conducting—first interviews. My clients typically have a trusted manager take on these responsibilities. You should also consult an employment attorney before making changes to your recruiting and job application process. You want to be sure that you're complying with all applicable federal and state laws.

Online Job Boards

Online job boards like Monster.com, CareerBuilder, and a myriad other sites are being challenged today by social media tools as the online recruiting tools of choice. However, recruiters will tell you that these sites are still important to the recruiting process. Monster, CareerBuilder, and others are essentially online matchmaking sites for employers and employees. Employers pay to post their open jobs and to have access to job applicants, while job seekers post their resumes for free. Employers also pay to search through the extensive resume database that these job boards have accumulated over time. One advantage that these sites provide is that they are known by and attract many job seekers.

Barbie Spear is director of human resources for Alliance Holdings, an employee-owned holding company that invests in industrial and commercial manufacturers across the country. Barbie uses Monster.com to fill many positions—including top executive roles—within the manufacturers that the Alliance Holdings owns. Her firm owned a manufacturing firm in Ohio that was consistently losing money. Barbie decided to try finding a new chief executive officer for the company on Monster before she called a headhunter. She posted the open position, received a number of resumes, sorted through them, and subsequently filled the job from among these applicants. The new CEO took the company from losing money to a significant before-tax profit. Not a bad return on a few hundred bucks spent to post an open position.

Will I Be Overwhelmed with Resumes?

One of the complaints about job boards is that they inundate you with resumes from unqualified people. This can be overwhelming, particularly if you don't have dedicated human resources staff to wade through them for you. To address this, major job boards allow you to screen and sort resumes using key words. If, for example, you want to hire a manufacturing engineer who knows how to reduce costs using Lean Manufacturing methods, you can sort resumes using "lean" as a criteria. Then, only resumes that contain this word will be sent to you. You can use this sorting capability in both job postings and resume database searches to save you time and pinpoint potential A-players.

By definition, job boards attract people who are at least *somewhat* active in seeking a new position. If you want to find and hire an A-player who is happily employed and not looking for a job (the so-called passive candidate), sites like Monster and CareerBuilder probably aren't the best places to find them. However, when you purchase the right to sort through the resume databases on these sites, you do have access to people who are employed now but were looking for a job some time ago. Recruiters tap into these databases all the time to build their contact lists, so there is no reason you can't do the same.

While there are countless other places you can go to find A-players these days, the major job boards still have their place in the process. They enable you to reach a large number of job seekers at a relatively low cost. Many internal recruiters feel that, for about

$400 for a single position, it is worth the time to sort through resumes to see if you can find some strong candidates.

> **A-Player Principle:** The big job boards like Monster and CareerBuilder still have their place in the A-player recruiting process. Use sort criteria and the other technology tricks these sites offer to reduce resume overload.

Additional Sites to Check Out

In addition to Monster and CareerBuilder, other employment sites to check out include HotJobs (www.hotjobs.yahoo.com) and The Ladders (www.theladders.com), a site that focuses on positions that pay at least six figures. Sites like www.indeed.com and www.simply-hired.com are employment search engines that scour job boards and web postings for positions that match the criteria of job seekers. These sites and others like them allow employers to register their open positions, often for free.

Industry-Specific Job Boards

One way to attract people with industry experience or a specific professional background is to use industry or expertise-specific job boards. For example, if you want to hire a chief financial officer or controller, you can post your job on the Financial Executives Networking Group web site (www.thefeng.org), on the Financial Executives International web site (www.financialexecutives.org), or on CFO.com (www.cfo.com). Most industries and disciplines have several job boards associated with them. Check out the web site of your own professional association—it likely provides similar forums at the local and national levels.

Craigslist

For $25 to $75, you can post a job on Craigslist (www.craigslist .org), the well-known online bazaar in which you can buy and sell almost anything. You are not going to fill an executive position this way, but if this site is used heavily in your city or town, it's another viable way to find applicants. Be ready, however, to wade through a number of applicants—including many who are completely unqualified.

I know business owners who wrote effective job posts on Craigslist, took the time to sort through all the applicants, and ultimately found an A-player. This can work particularly well if you intentionally craft the role to appeal to a specific talent pool, such as women reentering the workforce. This is one way to make a Craigslist posting work as part of your A-player strategy.

Social Media

As mentioned, job boards have been around for a long time, whereas social media tools that allow you to connect with a global network of people are the new wave of recruiting technology. Today, LinkedIn, Twitter, and Facebook are the three major social media tools that are receiving the most attention. Let's discuss how to make the most effective use of these sites in creating your A-player team.

What Is LinkedIn?

When you talk with recruiting professionals, you often hear about their use of LinkedIn (www.linkedin.com), a social networking tool that most people use for no cost. To join, you create an "online resume" that gives others a picture of your professional background. LinkedIn then allows you to upload your contacts and "connect" with these people and with others whom you meet through the multitude of LinkedIn member groups. These groups let members share ideas, establish virtual relationships, and expand their contacts. The goal of all this activity is to give you immediate access to a huge network of people. LinkedIn is a technological embodiment of "six degrees of separation," which says that you are only six people away from being able to connect with anyone on the planet.

I recently used LinkedIn regarding a new business opportunity. I received a notification from a business association looking for a keynote speaker. Given the professional speaking I do on creating A-player teams, it looked like an interesting opportunity. I didn't know anyone associated with the group. Its headquarters are located only 45 minutes from my office, however, so the chances were good that someone in my network was familiar with it. A quick search on the executive director's name through LinkedIn revealed that I was connected to several people who are also connected to this individual. (I would never have figured this out quickly without using LinkedIn.) I then followed up with two of these contacts to see what they knew about the person and the group. Neither of them knew much, but both volunteered to reach out to their contacts to see what they could learn. Within days I got their feedback—and it was not positive. My contacts' contacts had *nothing* good to say about this organization. As a result, I dropped this group as a prospective client for me.

In this situation, I was the potential "applicant" searching for information on the "employer." LinkedIn enabled me to figure out quickly which of my contacts were likely to be familiar with this organization and get reliable feedback on the group. This ability to pinpoint relevant contacts makes LinkedIn a powerful recruiting tool (and saved me from taking on a potentially problematic client).

> **A-Player Principle:** LinkedIn is the recruiter's tool of choice for quickly making contacts, checking references, and getting access to A-players. Once your own LinkedIn network is set up, you'll receive almost instant, no-cost insight into "who knows who."

Let's build on LinkedIn's capabilities by exploring several specific ways to use the system to find A-players.

Posting Jobs on LinkedIn

For $200 or less, you can post a job on LinkedIn. Individuals can apply for the position, and you can view their LinkedIn profile when they do so. Of course, these profiles are not audited by an outside source, so "buyer beware" of both the content of the resumes and the veracity of the testimonial statements.

Sending Direct Communication via LinkedIn

LinkedIn also provides the ability to send messages directly to people in your network. A vice president of human resources recently included me on a direct e-mail through LinkedIn. He was looking for a junior marketing person with three years of experience, strong communication and analytical skills, and the willingness to work long hours. He said in his note, "We've been scouring the resumes on the job board and are not able to use a search firm. Any thoughts or suggestions will be welcome." The position was too junior to justify paying a recruiting fee, and the job boards were coming up empty. But this executive had not given up hope. He went directly to his network via LinkedIn to see if he could scare up some good applicants.

Conducting Due Diligence on Job Candidates

Professional recruiters use LinkedIn to build their candidate lists, and you can do the same. For instance, a recruiter filling a pharmaceutical sales position will use LinkedIn to find contacts who work for one of the big pharmaceutical companies. From there, he will pare the list down to individuals who are currently in sales for these companies. Now the recruiter has a call list for finding the best candidates.

You may or may not be comfortable creating this kind of list and cold-calling potential candidates. However, LinkedIn can also be used to research candidates and check references. When a job candidate is referred to you, you can enter his or her name into the "Search People" field within LinkedIn. If that person uses LinkedIn, his or her public profile will pop up. In addition, a graphic appears on the lower-right-hand side of the page that shows how you are connected to this individual and also displays your common contacts. It looks like Figure 7.3:

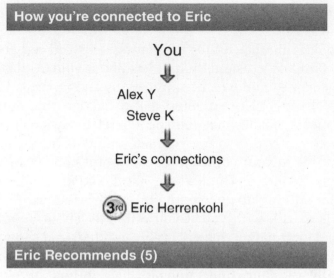

FIGURE 7.3   Connections on LinkedIn

This single graphic provides you with a great source of references for this person. While LinkedIn gives people the ability to post testimonials from their clients and associates in their profiles, don't depend on these statements. Instead, contact the people you know in common to obtain an honest reference on your job candidate.

A-Player Principle: Use LinkedIn to find people for your farm team as well as mutual connections who can tell you if these people are as good as they claim to be.

Facebook: Is a Candidate Giving You Reasons to Say No?

Facebook began as a tool for college kids to check one another out but has expanded to become *the* social networking choice of tool for countless individuals. While it is still primarily a tool for maintaining personal relationships, most professionals who actively use social media will have a Facebook profile, and many businesses have them as well.

Facebook is another means for getting the word out about your A-Player Profile. Occasional reminders about your A-player mind-set will generate employment applications and referrals from your Facebook "friends." Keep in mind that social decorum in the world of social media dictates that you spend a relatively small portion of your time directly promoting yourself and your business. Provide posts of value to your connections and point people toward valuable online resources. Think about Facebook and all social media as tools for striking up and conducting conversations. After all, no one wants to talk with you if you only talk about yourself. Post insight and information that is of value to others and show a sincere interest in what others have to say. This will earn you the right to periodically ask your connections for help to find an A-player for your business.

Like LinkedIn, Facebook can also be a tool for conducting due diligence on job candidates. But keep in mind that there are a couple of tricks here.

1. Significant access to someone's Facebook profile can be limited to his or her direct connections, so in some cases you can't check out someone's Facebook profile unless he or she approves you as a "friend."

2. Because Facebook is more personal than professional, some questions have been raised about the legality of viewing Facebook pages as part of the hiring process.

Having said this, if people do not have the good judgment to portray themselves appropriately on Facebook, will they have the good judgment to represent your company well?

A-Player Principle: Hiring is a numbers game, and there are huge numbers of people on Facebook. Get your Facebook friends to help you find A-players.

Twitter

Twitter is the leading social media site for a trend known as micro-blogging. In essence, it's a tool that allows you to post 140 character-messages to let others know "what you are doing." Twitter has become a powerhouse in social networking. Recruiters are using it to tap into broad networks of people with strong qualifications who may not be actively looking for a job.

Executive Director of Talent Tracy Cote and Director of Talent Acquisition Traci Armstrong both work for Organic, one of the United States' leading interactive marketing agencies. Organic has been an early adopter of Twitter in the recruiting world, with these executives leading the charge. They say, "If an interview is like a first date, then Twitter is like having several phone conversations before you meet face to face." Twitter allows users to develop a network of "followers" who read your 140-character "tweets." Organic has found that a key to using Twitter to find A-players is to develop a following among the people they want to recruit. As the recruiting leaders at Organic say: "Just building an unfocused network of people is not as helpful as building a following of individuals who work in the areas where you want to focus your recruiting efforts."

If, for example, you want to hire advertising agency account executives, you would find these people on Twitter and follow them. They, in turn, will often follow you. Then make sure to post information these people find valuable. "This means talking about a lot more than your open positions," according to the Organic team. "You have to talk about issues that people care about and that provide value for them—otherwise they won't pay any attention to you." Talk their language. Provide valuable perspective. Pass along links to worthwhile blogs. Organic's recruiters will even pass along noncompetitive job openings at other companies. The key is to provide focused, specific insight that potential A-players find valuable.

Twitter is a great way to strike up online conversations with A-players whom you've never met in person. When you engage with people this way, over time they can become genuine members of your professional network. Then, when you periodically let them know about your desire to hire A-players, you reach an enormous number of targeted people at no incremental cost. This ability to reach a large group of people that includes A-players is proving to be a game changer in the world of recruiting.

The Advantages of Twitter over Traditional Job Boards

Twitter offers some significant benefits compared to the more traditional job board sites. First of all, your job postings can "go viral." If your employees are on Twitter, they can pass along a job posting to their followers, who in turn pass them along to their followers if they are of interest. This exponentially increases the number of people that your job posting reaches.

In addition, Twitter allows you to reach more qualified applicants. If you and your team build a sizable Twitter following within your industry, you can generate a significant number of qualified responses to your job postings. Tracy Cote and Traci Armstrong estimate that 50 to 60 percent of job applicants obtained through Twitter are qualified versus 10 percent of the applicants generated from postings on major job boards. Recruiting is a numbers game, so this ability to generate a larger number of qualified candidates with limited incremental cost is *incredibly* powerful.

Organic rewards its employees for new hires made through social media referrals. It pays a $1,500 bonus when employees recommend someone who is hired and remains employed for at least 90 days. The company's employment application asks new hires who referred them, a name that the majority of new hires *do* know—even if it was a purely virtual referral. Organic welcomes paying these referral fees: it beats paying a headhunter's fee.

A-Player Principle: Some recruiters estimate that 50 to 60 percent of job applicants found through Twitter are qualified versus 10 percent of applicants found through major job boards. You can't ignore a recruiting tool that powerful.

Great, but How Do I Make This Work?

You may be thinking that it sounds great to include Twitter and these other tools in your recruiting process. But *realistically*, how do you make this work? Here are some suggestions.

Get Some Outside Help

A variety of individuals and companies provide social media consulting and coaching these days. Find a knowledgeable but reasonably priced person to help you get your social media infrastructure set up. Elance.com and guru.com are two sites that connect companies with independent contractors, and there are a large number of social media consultants and coaches to be found on these sites. Another source of good talent in this area is the International Virtual Assistants Association (www.ivaa.org/index.asp), as well as the local Virtual Assistants Association in your region. Virtual assistants are independent contractors who provide administrative services to companies. A subset of these service providers have developed strong skills in social media and can be of help.

Train Your Employees

If you are going to have your employees use social media to promote your company and find A-players, make sure that they use this technology appropriately. Establish guidelines. Provide training. Monitor activity. While there are some substantial potential benefits, there are also risks to promoting a grassroots social media campaign for your company. So be sure that you have thought these risks through and addressed them up front.

As this book is being written, the impact of social media on recruiting is creating reverberations in the world of employment law. Lawyers are now asking if companies that rely too much on Twitter for recruiting are excluding certain groups from access to jobs. You should be reaching out to A-players wherever and whenever you can find them. LinkedIn, Twitter, Facebook, and similar tools are powerful tools, but they are not the *only* tools for creating an A-player team. Don't rely on them exclusively any more than you would rely on just one means of acquiring new customers. Finally, run your recruiting strategy past an employment attorney to make sure you're doing things correctly.

All the online tools we have discussed are simply additional techniques for expanding your network and finding A-players. They don't take the place of building personal relationships, but they can accelerate the process. Social media is a very low-cost way to magnify your recruiting reach. You have to establish a presence there anyway; you might as well make it pay off in more quality hires!

A-Player Payoff Points

Chapter 7: The Basics of Online Recruiting

- Your company's web site is the anchor of your recruiting efforts, so make sure that it has an employment page that clearly expresses your A-Player Profile and emphasizes what your company has to offer A-players.
- Job boards like Monster and CareerBuilder still provide a strong return on investment. Use search and sort criteria to winnow down the number of resumes you receive. Why not pay $400 and see what you get *before* you pay a recruiter's fee?
- LinkedIn is a great tool for developing a contact list of A-players. It also helps you to find mutual contacts who will give you honest feedback on an applicant.
- Savvy professionals who use social media typically have a Facebook page. Use Facebook as another tool for connecting with people and generating A-player referrals.
- Twitter allows you to develop a following in your industry or specialty and "go viral" with job postings. It is changing the world of recruiting as we speak.
- Delegate responsibility for social media to someone in or out of your company who has expertise and interest in this area. You can get value from these tools without having to spend a lot of your own time.

8

Using Recruiters Wisely

A company that I do work for does a terrific job of finding and hiring A-players. It follows the steps in this book, has a strong farm team, and consistently hires A-players. Yet when the time came to find a new vice president of sales, the president of this company used an outside recruiting firm that specialized in sales and sales management. The president had several people on his farm team who were contenders for the role, but he wanted to conduct an exhaustive search that guaranteed the company hired the best person available. He was willing to pay a recruiting fee of 25 to 30 percent of first year starting salary. The recruiter conducted a thorough process, winnowed the candidates down to a final list—and the company hired its top choice.

Several years later, this new vice president of sales has been instrumental in taking this business to the next level of success. She is a great leader and is committed to creating a team of A-players. The recruiting fee this company incurred to find her has paid for itself many times over.

Ironically, it is often the companies that are effective at finding A-players on their own that turn to outside recruiters to fill leadership roles and key technical positions. Because these companies are so committed to creating an A-player team, they are willing to invest in recruiters' fees when necessary. No company wants to pay a recruiter 20 to 30 percent of first-year salary, but sometimes doing so is the right decision.

In contrast, companies that have not used recruiters often don't understand their value and are hesitant to use them. The chairman of a large, privately held construction firm told me that he found the idea of hiring an outside recruiter to be repugnant—until he talked to his friends in the Young Presidents' Organization and

---

A-Player Principle: Ironically, it is often the companies that know how to find and hire A-players that turn to outside recruiting firms to fill key roles. Their commitment to creating a team of A-players makes the recruiting fee worth it.

found that *all* of them had used these firms to fill important positions. This company chairman then decided to use a recruiter to fill a key role and was glad that he did.

When to Use Recruiters

The right recruiters are a valuable asset for finding A-players. You turn to recruiters when:

- You want to turn over every rock to make sure you find and hire the best person—whether the person is actively looking for a new position or not.
- You need very specific industry or technical expertise.
- You want to hire people out of certain companies but don't have the relationships with these individuals to reach them directly.
- You want to recruit someone from a competitor and prefer to have a middleman do it for you.
- The cost of allowing a position to go unfilled exceeds the cost of paying a recruiter's fee.

Finding the Right Recruiter

Outside recruiting firms find A-players on your behalf. They determine what you are looking for in a new hire and then reach out to their networks to find the people who best fit this profile. Once they identify these candidates, they present them to your company, and you make the final hiring decision. Contingency recruiting firms get paid if you hire a candidate that they present to you. Retained recruiting firms get paid for designing and executing a recruiting process. You pay them even if you don't hire one of their candidates.

There is an incredible range in the quality and sophistication of outside recruiters. High-end retained firms that fill senior executive roles have extremely structured processes for determining job descriptions, recruiting and interviewing candidates, and making final hiring decisions. Low-end contingency firms may do no more than have a phone conversation with you about the position you are filling, send you 10 resumes, and let you figure out the rest.

Headhunters are brokers. They achieve success when a deal has been sealed and your company hires their candidate. A few are fantastic. They listen to your needs, conduct a great process, watch out for your interests, and consistently find and place A-players. Others can perform poorly. They're more salespeople than recruiting experts, and they try to push any warm body to fill a position. As a result, if you choose to use recruiters—and I believe you should in certain cases—choose wisely. Select a recruiter with the care that you would use to select an attorney or CPA. When you find a good one, hold onto that relationship with everything that you have.

> **A-Player Principle:** There are situations in which paying a recruiting fee is well worth the cost. A good relationship with an effective recruiter can be a valuable asset in the struggle to find talent.

Criteria for Selecting a Recruiting Firm

How do you differentiate between great recruiters and average ones? Here are some characteristics the best recruiters share.

They Know Your Industry

You don't have to educate the best firms about your industry; they already understand it. Whether you work with a retained or contingent firm, you want to hire one that knows your field and understands how different roles and positions fit together in a company like yours. Justin Smith, a highly regarded recruiting executive in the retail industry, says, "The best recruiters not only know the right people. They understand what those people do and how they fit into your organizational strategy. For example, a recruiter may know a lot of people who are Java programmers. But do they understand how a Java programmer fits into your IT department and what differentiates a great programmer from an average one? That is the kind of knowledge that differentiates great recruiters from everyone else."

A company I know recently hired a search firm to fill a chief information officer position with responsibility for global operations. The recruiter it retained had just successfully completed a similar CIO search for another company in this industry. The search went very well, in large part because the recruiter already knew the relevant players and was ready to conduct an effective search.

They Listen

The best recruiters take the time to understand what you are trying to accomplish and whom you need. Particularly for lower-level positions (annual compensation less than $100,000 per year), some firms are notorious for "throwing spaghetti at the wall" and seeing what sticks. That is *not* what you want from a recruiting firm—no matter what position you're seeking to fill. You want a recruiter who will strategize with you to define your A-Player Profile and then focus on finding people who fit those criteria.

They Have a Transparent Process

The process is the product when it comes to good recruiting. Particularly in a retained search, the best firms map out every individual with whom they speak and review this list with you. As the client, this gives you the opportunity to make sure the recruiter is casting a wide net and reaching a lot of qualified people. You can then see in detail how the recruiting firm uses your agreed-on A-Player Profile to narrow the search to a short list of the best people. Some recruiting firms resist this kind of transparency, but it adds value and provides peace of mind for you.

They Are Good Ambassadors for Your Business

An outside recruiter becomes the face of your business to every person with whom they speak, so make sure that you hire a recruiter who represents you well. Many recruiters are aggressive and sales-oriented, and it is great to have such people working on your behalf. Just make sure that your recruiter is also professional, intelligent, and trustworthy.

You Have a Relationship Based on Trust

The best recruiters are worth their weight in gold. You will likely have to work hard to find one or two great ones. So when you do find these people, cultivate those relationships for the long term. Make sure that the recruiters you hire are people with whom you can see this kind of relationship developing. If you don't have a good feeling about them, find another firm.

Contingent versus Retained Recruiters

Should you use a contingent or a retained recruiter to fill your key position? Here are some suggestions on when each is appropriate.

Contingent Recruiters

For positions that pay less than $100,000 annually, recruiters typically work on a contingent arrangement in which they are paid only if you hire a candidate that they find for you. You'll want to use these firms to find candidates when your company can oversee the screening and interviewing process on its own. Contingent firms typically:

- Take a somewhat less structured approach to defining the requirements of the job.
- Focus more on candidate "sourcing." They find qualified candidates for your company and then allow you to take over the screening and interviewing process to select the right person.

> **A-Player Principle:** Use contingent firms when your company is prepared to oversee the interview process while the outside recruiter sources candidates for you.

Retained Recruiters

Retained recruiting firms focus on executive (six figures and up) positions. These firms typically provide a search process that includes:

- Face-to-face interviews with your team to define the role that you are filling.
- Mapping out and contacting potential candidates for the role.
- Keeping you updated on the candidates they have contacted.
- Screening and interviewing candidates.
- Providing you with a relatively small number of qualified candidates to interview.

When you talk with references for these firms, make sure to verify the thoroughness and effectiveness of their recruiting process. At the end of a search, you want to feel confident that your recruiter did everything possible to find and hire the right A-player for your company. Ryan Lafferty is one of the founders of Attolon Partners, a firm that provides retained search for accounting, finance, and information technology executives. In Ryan's words, "There should be steady reporting and updates on the direction of the search and on the specific candidates reached throughout the search process. That kind of process gives clients peace of mind. It's a large part of the value of retained search."

Having made these distinctions, the best contingent firms often act like retained firms. They take the time to listen to you at the beginning of the process and understand the position you are filling. They have deep contacts in your industry that allow them to reach out and comprehensively search for the strongest candidates. They also emphasize finding *qualified* candidates rather than just sending you resumes.

A-Player Principle: The best recruiters combine a proven process for uncovering A-players with deep contacts and industry knowledge. When you interview recruiters, look for all three factors.

Specialists versus Generalists

You are generally better off working with a recruiter who specializes in your industry or discipline. If you are hiring salespeople for the pharmaceutical industry, there are recruiters who specialize in that role. If you are hiring petrochemical engineers, there are recruiters who focus on filling just such positions. If you are hiring a chief financial officer or controller, there are firms that do nothing but place financial executives.

Specialization makes sense when you realize that recruiters spend every day talking to people who are both potential clients (executives who want to hire someone) and potential candidates (individuals interested in the right new opportunity). The more recruiters focus on a specific industry or job type, the deeper their contacts and understanding become. This translates into a recruiter who quickly grasps what you need in your new hire and efficiently taps into a strong network of people to find the right A-player for your business.

There are recruiting firms out there that are generalists. These firms are one-stop shops; they will fill almost any position in your company. If you build a strong relationship with a firm like this, it can become the outsourced recruiting department of your company. This can be a valuable solution, but be cautious when you first try to establish such a relationship. If you have limited experience with recruiting firms, your tendency will be to turn to a recruiter you know from your network. When you ask the recruiter if he or she can fill any position—from chief executive to dog catcher—the recruiter will likely say "Absolutely." In most situations, you are better off being referred to a recruiter who specializes in your industry or area of need. You will likely have more success finding the next A-player for your organization with specialists.

> **A-Player Principle:** Though there are exceptions, you typically want a recruiter who specializes in your industry or discipline rather than a generalist. Don't pay a recruiter to learn your business; leverage those who already have the knowledge and contacts that you need.

Hire the Recruiter, Not the Firm

Some great advice for college students is to "take the professor, not the class." A terrific professor can transform a seemingly boring subject into something interesting and valuable, while a lousy professor can turn the most scintillating topic into a trip through Purgatory. This same wisdom applies when hiring a recruiter. Hire the recruiter, not the firm. The outside recruiter you select may work for one of the biggest search firms in the world or for a boutique firm with a small staff. Hiring a big firm does not guarantee you great results. Find a recruiter who is well known and well respected in your niche and make sure that he or she will personally conduct your search. The size of his or her firm is secondary.

> **A-Player Principle:** Bigger does not necessarily mean better in the world of recruiting. Find the individual recruiters with the best reputations, regardless of the size of the firms for which they work.

Checklist for Interviewing Recruiters

When you find a handful of reputable recruiters in your space, interview them before hiring one. Here are some questions to ask:

- What industries or roles do you specialize in? (Are they generalists or specialists?)
- How many searches have you conducted in our industry in the past year? (Do they have the industry expertise you want?)
- How many positions have you filled in these areas in the past year? (Do they have a deep list of contacts as a result of recent search activity?)
- Can you describe your process for conducting this kind of search? (Listen for how comprehensive and analytical their procedure sounds to you. Is this a recruiter who is going to

follow a great process or a firm that shoots from the hip? Clearly, you want the former.)

- What is your success rate? (Believe it or not, many searches are unsuccessful—the positions don't get filled.)
- Who will be conducting my search? (Particularly in large recruiting firms, well-known search consultants are the rainmakers, while less seasoned consultants conduct the searches. Make sure you know whom you are hiring.)
- What is your fee for this kind of search? Is it calculated on base salary, base plus bonus, or some other formula? Do you have any flexibility in your fee schedule?
- What type of guarantee do you have for candidates that you place? (Almost every firm provides some sort of guarantee for the placements it makes. If a candidate placed by a search firm leaves within the guarantee period, some firms provide a pro-rated reimbursement of your fee. Other firms redo the search at no additional fee. The time frame of these guarantees differ, so verify that as well.)
- Who are your clients? (A very important question, because firms *will not* recruit employees from their current clients. If the people you want to hire work for a recruiter's clients, forget that firm and find its best competitor.)
- Can you provide me with at least five executive references at companies where you have conducted a search in the past year? (Make sure to check them.)
- What taxes must be paid on your search fees? (Depending on the state in which the firm is based, you may be responsible to pay taxes on the recruiting fees. While this shouldn't be your number-one criterion for choosing a firm, it is good to know).

Check Recruiters' References

Just as when you hire an employee, checking references burns up time but is *always* worth it in the end. You will deal with this recruiter extensively, and he or she will represent your company in the marketplace. It's worth your time to verify that a recruiter generates good results and "plays well with others."

Matt Todt, a seasoned recruiting manager in the pharmaceutical industry, asks these questions when speaking to a recruiter's references:

- Is this recruiter professional?
- Does the recruiter follow up and do what he or she promised?
- Does the recruiter have a well-defined process for conducting a search?
- Does the recruiter follow instructions?
- Did the recruiter interact with you and your people appropriately, or was he or she inappropriately aggressive?
- Would you hire the recruiter again?

Negotiating the Contract

The process is not over when you settle on a recruiting firm. You want to review the contract closely before you sign it and have your attorney do so as well. Here is another helpful checklist from Matt Todt to guide your contract negotiation with a recruiting firm.

- What is the fee? Calculated on base salary? Base plus bonus?
- What is the guarantee period?
- What is the definition of a "candidate"? For example, you can stipulate that if a recruiting firm presents you with a candidate who is already in your database, you don't owe that firm a fee if you hire the person. Alternatively, if a recruiter submits someone to your company and you hire him or her later for a different role, you often still pay the recruiter's fee.
- Include nonsolicitation and confidentiality agreements in the contract. These are clauses that spell out that the recruiting firm cannot recruit your employees or share information with your competitors. Ethical firms always follow these guidelines, but it never hurts to have them in writing.
- In order to fulfill a guarantee, recruiting firms sometimes require written details about why a new hire they placed with a company did not work out. You can take this verbiage out of

the agreement if you don't want to provide this information to an outside party.

- Confirm what state sales tax (if any) must be paid on search fees.

> **A-Player Principle:** Pay attention to the details of your recruiting contract. Follow the checklists in this chapter to avoid unpleasant surprises down the road.

A Word about Fees

Recruiting fees typically range from 20 to 30 percent of first-year starting salary, plus any additional expenses the recruiter incurs during the search. I once worked with a contingent recruiter who occasionally agreed to work at reduced fees with clients who negotiated. He made 30 percent of starting salary with Company A and 20 percent with Company B. Company B thought it had driven a great bargain with him, but it did not account for the fact that it was always the second client to interview the A-players he recruited. This recruiter sent his strongest candidates first to the companies that paid full fees.

You don't have to pay absolute top dollar to recruiters, but you must be willing to pay a competitive rate. A firm that takes a bargain-basement fee arrangement is often desperate for business and will likely not represent your firm well in the marketplace. You do get what you pay for when it comes to recruiters.

Lessons Learned from the Best Recruiters

There are times when you should hire an outside recruiting firm. However, the primary point of this book is that you and your team must take responsibility for finding and hiring A-players. What can you learn from the best recruiters about how to find A-players? Here are some takeaways.

Ask for Referrals Constantly

I know a recruiter who asks every individual whom she places with a new company for a phone directory from his or her former employer. When she gets it, she immediately gets on the phone to expand her own network of contacts. While you don't have to be quite as aggressive, you should be asking people for A-player referrals *all the time*. Particularly when you hire new A-players, strategize with them about connecting with other A-players in their networks.

The Internet Is Not a Replacement for Networking

Karyn Rogers Verret, president of Verret & Associates, a well-regarded executive search firm in the retail industry, strongly believes that "the Internet is a supplement to—not a replacement for—personal contact." You should absolutely leverage social media tools to make initial contacts, but you build those connections into relationships via phone and face-to-face contact with people.

Cast a Wide Net

As an executive committed to hiring A-players, the more people you meet, interview, and add to your farm team, the better your chances of having A-players to hire when you want them. The best outside searches for A-players start with hundreds of possible candidates and narrow down to a handful of highly qualified people. Doing this yields multiple candidates who have strong technical qualifications. Then, the company doing the hiring can focus on selecting the person who combines this technical ability with critical leadership skills, communication skills, and potential for further promotions.

The Process Is King

The best search firms emphasize the quality and thoroughness of their recruiting process. They know that it is their ability to conduct an exhaustive search every time that keeps their clients coming back. If your company is committed to hiring A-players, you must pledge to make recruiting a strong, ongoing process, not a haphazard and periodic event.

A-Player Payoff Points

Chapter 8: Using Recruiters Wisely

- Companies that are great at hiring Λ-players on their own often use outside recruiters to fill key positions. They value what the best recruiters bring to the table and use them appropriately.
- In the recruiting world, there are used-car salespeople and incredibly effective professionals. Interview recruiters as you would job candidates. Hold on for dear life to the good ones when you find them.
- Find a recruiter who understands your industry and has recently conducted successful searches similar to yours. You want to leverage a recruiter's experience and contacts, not educate him or her about the basics of your business.
- The right executive recruiter is like any other professional advisor. You will get a lot more value from these people if you know, like, and trust them. Find someone with whom you can be open about your business's strengths and weaknesses.
- When using contingent recruiters, be prepared to oversee the interview process yourself. These recruiters typically are focused on sourcing qualified people, not vetting the people they find.
- A retained search firm should be transparent with you about the individuals with whom it is speaking as part of your search. You should have the peace of mind that comes from knowing that the firm is turning over every rock to find your company an A-player.

(continued)

(*continued*)

- In general, specialists are better than generalists when it comes to recruiting firms. Specializing gives recruiters deep knowledge and deep contacts, both of which help them to find you the best people.
- Hire the recruiter, not the firm. In addition, make sure that you don't get handed off to a junior recruiter after you sign a contract with a recruiting firm.
- Learn from the best recruiters. Constantly build your network and your farm team before you need them, so that you have A-players to hire when you want them.

Interviewing and the Economic Value of Good Looks

As a friend of mine says, never underestimate the economic power of good looks. It's no secret that we all tend to pay attention to attractive people. Researcher and writer Kate Lorenz says, "Studies show attractive students get more attention and higher evaluations from their teachers, good-looking patients get more personalized care from their doctors, and handsome criminals receive lighter sentences than less-attractive convicts."[1] Yet we all know that just because someone looks good, acts confidently, and communicates well does not mean that he or she will perform well. That is why it is so important to create an interview process that helps you to look beneath a person's surface to his or her accomplishments, strengths, and weaknesses.

A-Players Are Attracted by High Standards

An executive I know recently interviewed for and accepted a leadership role with a new company. As part of the interview process, the company required him to engage in multiple interviews and a series of leadership and management assessments. The human resources person who was his liaison with this company apologized for how much time the whole process took. His reply was telling: "Please don't apologize. I think this whole process is terrific. It communicates to me that you are serious about hiring the best leaders you can find for this company." Far from being put off by the demanding interview process, he was *attracted* by it. He subsequently took the job this company offered to him.

A-players are drawn to organizations with high standards. Design an interview process that digs into people's accomplishments, talents, and experiences. A-players prefer stringent interviews as long as the questions, assessments, and overall method are job related. They like to jump through these hoops because they look good doing it. It allows them to show off their skills and be recognized by a new group of people for their abilities. In this sense, a demanding interview process is a recruiting tool that attracts A-players.

> **A-Player Principle:** A-players are attracted by high standards. Don't apologize for conducting a rigorous interview process. The best candidates like to feel they are joining an exclusive club when they join your team.

Create an Interview Process that Works

When I worked as an executive recruiter, my clients were the chief executives and chief financial officers of some well-regarded companies. It always surprised me that such successful people were lousy interviewers. They were so busy that they reviewed resumes for 30 seconds before meeting a candidate. They asked their questions and formed an impression of the candidate. Later, they ran into one of their colleagues in the hall and asked that perennial post-interview question: "So, what did you think of that guy?" That was the extent of their interview process. These executives made decisions based solely on gut feel and first impressions, instead of following a systematic process to hire the right person.

I am going to describe a series of steps that you can include in your interview process, but whatever you do, have *some* kind of system for it. A defined interview process gives you the insight you need to make good hiring decisions. We get better at what we do repeatedly, so follow that same process every time you interview. You and your organization will become well versed in choosing good hires if you develop a systematic interview process—and stick to it.

Always Start with Your A-Player Profile

One of the best things you can do to improve your interview process is to define your A-Player Profile (discussed in Chapter 2) before you conduct your first interview. If you want to stop settling for mediocre talent, then you must first clearly define superior performance. The A-Player Profile is the foundation of a great interview process. Take the time to create these Profiles for key positions and make sure that you and your people have bought into them. This will help you to say no to average performers and to recognize superior performers when you see them.

Capture and Quantify Your A-Player Profile

As I will discuss in Chapter 10, there are terrific personnel assessments out there that measure both the requirements of a job and a candidate's likelihood of being an A-player. If you capture and quantify your A-Player Profile using these tools, you can then compare job candidates to the Profile and see their strengths and weaknesses. These tools make interviewing more focused and effective. They help you to stay objective about people, weed out those who look good but lack substance, and focus on A-players you might otherwise have missed.

> **A-Player Principle:** Define your A-Player Profile before you interview anyone! Then, capture and quantify this Profile with a proven assessment tool so you can weed out mediocre talent and focus on the A-players.

Create an Interview Scorecard

Once you have defined success for the position and created the benchmark just described, you can quickly construct an interview scorecard. This does not need to be anything fancy. One entrepreneur I know has a simple card printed up with the five characteristics his company looks for when hiring for a sales position. Every interviewer gives candidates a score from one to five for each characteristic, as well as an overall score using the same scale. This helps the interviewers focus on issues that connect with job performance, judge every candidate according to the same criteria, and compare their impressions of candidates with those of the other interviewers.

Conduct Multiple Interviews

It's best to interview each serious candidate more than once and to conduct these interviews on at least two or three separate days. The interview is an artificial process designed to help you get to know a complete stranger quickly and in depth. You want to know whether people follow through on their commitments, communicate effectively via the phone and e-mail, and know how to get results. Meeting with them on different days will allow you to see if people write thank-you notes, show up on time for subsequent interviews, and remain enthusiastic about working for you. You can't begin to get all of this insight in just one day of interviews.

> **A-Player Principle:** Conduct multiple interviews over several different days to see if candidates follow up and follow through.

Use Multiple Interviewers

Goldman Sachs is legendary for having 20 to 30 people interview a candidate before he or she is hired. Before it was acquired by Macy's, May Department Stores interviewed every candidate for assistant buyer nine times, and many of these interviews included multiple interviewers. You make better hiring decisions when you involve multiple interviewers in the process. If you can, involve all the interviewers in the creation of the A-Player Profile. Involvement creates buy-in. If the interviewers participate in defining the requirements of the job, often they are more committed to making sure that the people they interview meet these requirements. Multiple interviewers provide you with multiple points of view. You want as many opinions as is feasible when you are making hiring decision.

Create Interviewing Teams

In general, interviewing candidates with a partner is preferable to doing so alone. When the other person asks the candidate a question, you can listen intently to the answers. In addition, the right interview partner will focus on different issues than you do and, as a result, catch things about the candidate that you might miss.

Team up with people who approach issues differently than you do. If, for example, you are a people-oriented person and make quick, impulsive decisions, then partner with a cool, analytical type who has a data-driven decision-making style. That person's tendency to focus on facts, not personality, will balance well with your propensity to concentrate on personality and intangibles. Conversely, if you are an analytical type, then you'll want to team up with someone who has a strong ability to build rapport quickly with people. His or her personable approach will help to get the candidate talking and elicit more data for you to use in making your hiring decision.

In a team interview, not only do you get to listen to the candidate's responses to your partner's questions, you can ask correlated questions that probe for the candidate's real accomplishments. Follow-up questions like "Why did you do that?" or "What would have been another way to handle that?" are some of the most important queries in an interview. This tandem interview process sets you up to ask them effectively.

> **A-Player Principle:** Conduct potential employee interviews with a partner. He or she will catch insights that you miss. After this happens a few times, you will never want to conduct an interview by yourself again.

Interview Candidates, Don't Educate Them

A director of sales was frustrated by the fact that her boss was always more impressed with certain sales candidates than she was. She interviewed these people when they first came into the office and did not find them to be all that remarkable. Then other sales managers interviewed each candidate. Finally, the candidate met with her superior, the senior vice president, at the end of the day. By that time, the interviewees really knew how to sell themselves and wowed her boss. Why?

It turned out that that the other sales managers were spending too much time talking about the company and not enough time asking good questions. Instead of digging into people's past sales accomplishments, these interviewers were educating job candidates about the company and its industry. Being salespeople, the candidates used this information to hone their personal sales pitches. To remedy this situation, the company moved to a team interview approach. It controlled the questions that were asked and the amount of information that was provided to job candidates early in the interview process. This helped to reduce its hiring mistakes.

There is a time and place in the recruitment process for educating people about your organization, but make sure not to overdo it early in the interview process. Make job candidates do their homework. Don't do it for them.

Ask the Right Questions

Open-ended questions always trump closed-ended questions in the interview process. Take a look at these two sample interview questions and ask yourself how effective they are. In this case, the hiring manager wants to probe into a candidate's leadership skills.

Open-Ended Question

"Tell me about a time when you had to lead your team in a new direction." Candidates will have to provide you with one or more challenges that they faced and the specific steps they took with their team to meet them. It will be clear to you if they fudge their answer and if the experience is genuine.

Closed-Ended Question

"Do you consider yourself to be a leader?" This question lets candidates off the hook by allowing them to give a one-word (or at least very limited) answer. You have learned nothing.

Unlike mutual funds, people's past performance *is* the best indicator of their future results. A simple but powerful approach to interviewing is to use open-ended questions to get people talking about their accomplishments at every stage of their life and career. If you ask the questions correctly, you will obtain an accurate picture of what they've achieved up to this point. Then you can decide if they are likely to realize the results you want from your next hire.

> **A-Player Principle:** A well-conducted interview always focuses on getting people to elaborate in detail about their past accomplishments. Use open-ended questions to encourage a conversation, not just yes-and-no answers.

Always Ask Follow-Up Questions

Even when you ask open-ended questions about people's accomplishments, you often receive rehearsed answers. Don't just accept these responses and move on. Always ask one or more follow-up questions.

Dr. Kurt Einstein was an executive recruiter who conducted research on interviewing techniques. One of Einstein's key points was that follow-up questions force job candidates to reveal if there is any substance behind their initial programmed responses. If candidates can describe in living detail how they accomplished something, they are likely telling the truth. If they provide broad-brush generalities in response to repeated follow-up questions, they are probably embellishing their achievements or overemphasizing their role in some way.

Using follow-up questions makes your job as an interviewer easier, since there are as many follow-up questions as there are accomplishments to discuss. You can simply ask about specific accomplishments and then follow up with "Tell me more" and "Why so?" and run a very effective interview. In addition, you can ask questions such as:

- "Why did you choose that strategy?"
- "What made you believe that layoffs were the right answer?"
- "What steps did you take to make purchasing more efficient?"
- "What specific things did you do to reduce the time to close the books from 30 days to 7 days?"

This tactic puts less pressure on you to come up with a lot of "creative" interview questions. Instead, you spend your time listening. If you follow this simple approach, you will conduct a strong interview every time.

> **A-Player Principle:** The most important question to ask in an interview is the follow-up question. Don't let candidates get away with just providing their rehearsed answers to your inquiries about their past accomplishments.

Case Study: Follow-Up Questions Work

While helping a client interview for a director of branch operations position, I saw a perfect example of why follow-up questions are so important. There were three candidates in the final interview process. We asked them to describe how they had taken underperforming branches and made them profitable. Then we dug into their initial answers with follow-up questions.

The first two candidates provided fine answers to our questions by giving specific examples of times when they replaced managers or rolled up their own sleeves to improve how these business units were run. The third candidate provided answers that were dramatically more systematic and detailed than the other two. He described, step by step, the processes that he taught his managers to follow in order to hit their financial goals. He also had multiple, specific examples of strategies he used to improve all aspects of branch operations.

My client hired the third candidate in large part because of his comprehensive responses to our follow-up questions. When he got on the job, he proved to be as effective as his answers were.

A-Player Principle: A-players can give you detailed, step-by-step descriptions of how they achieved past results. Don't hire people who can only answer in generalities and broad-brush responses.

Don't Be Afraid of Silence

Most people who conduct job interviews are scared of silence. If more than three seconds go by in which no one speaks, they rush in to fill the void. Don't do that. Ask a good question; ask a follow-up question; then close your mouth and force the candidate to talk. I once worked with an investment banker who was very effective at getting job candidates (and everyone else) to provide him with the information he wanted. He would ask a question and then sit silently for 30 seconds or longer until the other person spoke. In a job interview, as in life, you learn when you listen, not when you talk.

Take Notes

Try to take fairly thorough notes during an interview. You won't be able to write down every word, but do record key replies and phrases *in the candidate's own words*. When you go back to review your notes, these verbatim quotes will jog your memory better than your own version of their statements.

Implement a Post-Interview Review

I emphasize the importance of a post-interview review to evaluate job candidates. Meet with the other interviewers to discuss your observations as soon as possible after you complete an interview. When you team interview, it's usually pretty easy to take a few minutes afterward to compare notes with your partner. Make sure to go through this process with all the other interviewers as well. One interviewer will almost always catch an important point that everyone else missed. Taking the time to hold this session will reduce your chances of making hiring mistakes.

> **A-Player Principle:** Take notes during an interview and write down exact words and phrases that candidates use to answer your questions. Use these notes during the post-interview review to remind yourself of the candidate's strengths and weaknesses.

Avoid Hiring in Your Own Image

We tend to like people who remind us of ourselves. If you are hiring your successor and you personally are a terrific fit for your current role, then go ahead and hire your clone. However, most positions require people with skill sets that are complementary, not identical, to your own. When interviewing, focus on what the job requires, not just on whether you feel a natural affinity for the person.

Leverage Reference Checks

Brad Smart points out in his book *Topgrading* that when job candidates know you are going to speak with their former supervisors when you check their references, they have a greater incentive to be truthful in an interview.[2] Tell candidates up front that you will call all their past employers and want to speak with their direct supervisors. Have them provide you with their names and contact information and give you written permission to make these contacts. Ask them directly what you are likely to hear from their past bosses about their performance. If you are willing to be this candid, candidates are more likely to be open with you about their past failures or shortcomings.

Put People at Ease in a Casual Setting

An executive I know recently interviewed for a new position. He flew in for a series of weekend interviews with this company, and his wife joined him to look at houses in the area. On Sunday morning, the couple had breakfast with the senior vice president to whom he would report—along with her husband, her three sons, another company employee, and that employee's spouse. This senior executive was trying to impress this candidate and entice him to take this new position. She was also seeing how he acted and reacted in a social versus a professional setting.

For most people, looking good in business casual clothes actually takes more thought and effort than looking good in a suit. In the same way, it can be more work for people to create a favorable impression in a social setting than in a professional one. Get people out of your office or conference room and into a restaurant, company party, or sports event. Observe how the candidates interact with everyone. When people get comfortable, their game faces come off—and you get more insight into who they really are. While these are laid-back events, you should have a game plan for these situations. Have people on your team engage with candidates, ask them questions, and become acquainted with them. The person you get to know in this setting is the person you are actually hiring.

A-Player Principle: Get job candidates out of your office and into social settings. It's hard for people to keep their game face on and defenses up in these situations. This helps you to get a better sense of the person you are hiring.

Don't Oversell

Many executives enjoy the thrill of the hunt, and the recruiting process is all about capturing A-players. However, don't get so caught up in this excitement that you oversell the opportunity you have to offer. Several executives I know are as explicit about explaining a position's *drawbacks* to applicants as they are about explaining its strengths. These drawbacks can include:

- Extensive travel.
- Long hours or hours that extend beyond typical business hours.
- Limits on compensation in the first one to two years of employment.
- A relatively long ramp-up period to build a client base.

Be honest about these and similar issues. You want people to self-select out of the recruiting process if they are not willing to pay the cost required to be successful. Unfortunately, there will be people who are not able or willing to take themselves out of contention. You have to screen these people out yourself. A-players, however, often have a realistic grasp of the pluses and minuses of a job and still accept it. These are the people you want to hire.

"Live-Fire" Interview Exercises

Live-fire interview exercises centered on job-related skills can help to determine whether candidates will be successful in a particular role. These exercises provide candidates with the opportunity to display their skills in real time during the interview process. These simulations do not need to be complicated, but they should focus on skills that are relevant to the position. See how people think, communicate, and respond under pressure. Then incorporate this data into the hiring decision.

Some case studies that describe how clients have used these exercises to inform their hiring decisions are presented next.

Case Study: Can You Visualize a Blueprint?

I work with a number of companies in design-related industries, including architecture and home remodeling. Within this group are the members of the National Kitchen and Bath Association, which represents a range of organizations involved in the manufacture, design, and construction of residential kitchens and baths.

A kitchen and bath designer is a unique kind of salesperson. In addition to being able to sell, he or she must design and manage construction projects. I helped one client create a simple blueprint test to administer to candidates for this designer position. During the interview process, each candidate is asked to review a simple blueprint of a kitchen, make some basic measurements, and then indicate the proper dimensions of the designated cabinetry.

This very straightforward test pinpoints skills that some people just don't have: the ability to visualize a blueprint in three dimensions and read measurements accurately. By requiring every job candidate to complete this simple test, my clients weed out people who may have the interpersonal skills for the job but don't have the underlying technical competencies to be effective.

Case Study: Create a Sales Presentation for the Last Product You Sold

Another company that I know has a terrific business-to-business sales force. During the interview process, this company requires sales candidates to create a brief PowerPoint sales presentation focused on whatever product or service they sold in their *last* position. The company provides candidates with a computer and 30 minutes in which to build this presentation. Then the candidates deliver their pitch to the sales management team.

(continued)

(*continued*)

During the presentation, the sales managers raise objections and ask questions to see how candidates respond under pressure.

This exercise makes people put their sales skills on display. Do they communicate with confidence? Do they know how to sell value and results versus simply focusing on features and price? Are they prepared to answer objections? Do they know how to move the sales process forward and maintain momentum? Do they close well and ask for the business? Hiring managers can see all of these factors in action during this live-fire exercise. In addition, fundamental skills such as the ability to think logically and communicate concisely are also on display. Experienced sales managers can tell a lot about a candidate after just the first few slides of his or her presentation.

A subtle but important point here is that candidates are being asked to pitch the *last* product or service that they sold. They have no excuse for not being up to speed on what they are selling; they should already know those things cold. This is a great exercise that gives you another way to evaluate candidates beyond sitting behind a desk and asking them questions.

A-Player Principle: Don't just ask people if they can sell; have them prove it by pitching for their last product or service. Then pepper them with questions to see if they know their stuff and can perform well under pressure.

Case Study: Are You an Effective Buyer?

In retail stores, the ability to manage inventory and make consistently good buying decisions is critical to business success. One retail chain that I work with looks for employees who are effective with customers and can grow into a buyer role. To test their skills for the latter role, we created a role play. The hiring manager plays a vendor who is showing her company's new line of products to the buyer, played by the job candidate. The candidate must quickly sort through the different products being sold and make decisions about which ones to carry. She is then asked to explain her rationale for her recommendations. Finally, the candidate must put together a simple Excel spreadsheet that indicates how many units of each product will be purchased and how these purchases fit into the store's overall buying strategy.

This test helps the store manager to see candidates' decision-making skills in action. Do they make good decisions? Are their thought processes logical? Do they combine a good aesthetic sense with good business sense? Of course, you can and should ask questions in the interview that get at these issues. But why not create an exercise where you can *see* these abilities (or the lack thereof) right in front of your eyes?

A-Player Principle: The best interviews use multiple data sources to make informed hiring decisions. Use live-fire exercises to get to know job candidates more thoroughly.

Take Candidates with You

Another great way to see job candidates in action is to take them along with you during the course of your business day. Observe how they handle the tasks and interpersonal communication that are a part of your everyday experience. This extended time together gives you valuable insight into how people will operate after they are hired.

When Tom McKendry (executive tailor for Tom James Company, introduced in Chapter 5) is considering a new person for a sales position, he will take a serious candidate along with him on client visits *for two full days*. He instructs the candidate to ask his clients whatever he or she wants about Tom James and the products and service it provides. This approach:

- Is a great recruiting tool. Tom's confidence in his client relationships shines as he gives sales candidates access to these people.
- Provides candidates with the chance to get to know the company and understand the unique opportunities that Tom James provides to its people.
- Allows Tom to see people in action over the course of two days. As he says, "It's hard for candidates to keep their game faces on for that long."

> **A-Player Principle:** Companies that do the best job of hiring A-players do so *slowly*. They know that the more time you spend with someone, the harder it is for that person to fool you.

Have Candidates Make a Sales Call

A medical products sales manager I know actually sends final candidates out on sales calls by themselves before he hires them. He arranges to have them call on doctors he knows well. Each potential salesperson makes a presentation and tries to close a sale, or at least move the sales process forward. After each appointment, the manager calls the doctor and asks for feedback. If he hears that a candidate was overly nervous, lacked confidence, or was unable to lead the doctor to make a buying decision, that counts negatively against the person.

This is an admittedly high-intensity hiring test that not every company would or should use. But consider this: if you avoid hiring just one bad salesperson through this kind of process, how much money, aggravation, and lost opportunity have you saved?

> **A-Player Principle:** If these exercises sound like too much hassle to implement, just consider the wasted time, lost money, aggravation, and heartache that you incur every time you have to fire someone.

The Paid Interview

Vita Burdi, vice president at DJ's Home Improvements (introduced in Chapter 6), has taken the interview process to the next level by conducting what she calls a "paid interview." When Vita likes a candidate, she often asks the person to work for a few (paid) hours doing tasks similar to the ones he or she would be hired to do. Vita feels that in the matter of an hour or two, she and her managers can determine if these people are worth hiring. Do they jump in enthusiastically? Do they catch on quickly? Do they communicate well? Can they multitask? Instead of just relying on a standard interview to answer these questions, Vita allows people to prove their skills to her.

Be careful on this one. Talk with an employment attorney to make sure that your implementation of this exercise doesn't create any liability for your company.

> **A-Player Principle:** Figure out how you can spend time working side by side with people before you hire them. Interviewing this way helps to remove a lot of the guesswork about how effective they will be as employees.

Have Them Create an Action Plan

A company that I work with requires final candidates for sales positions to create an action plan for their first 90 days on the job *before* they are hired. At this point in the interview process, the candidates know a lot about the company, its products, and its customers—as much as they will their first day on the job. Why not see if they can take this information and create a realistic, results-oriented business plan? The vice president of sales reviews the plans with these questions in mind:

- **Did they complete the assignment?** Some people fail to execute this plan on time—or at all. If candidates can't hit a deadline during the interview process, what are the chances they will follow through on projects after you hire them?
- **Do they understand what it takes to succeed?** Investment precedes return in every conceivable role. Does this plan demonstrate a willingness to do what it takes to get the job done?
- **Are they specific?** The best action plans are explicit, detailed, and ready to execute. Is this person's plan detailed enough to actually implement, or is it so broad that it is really no plan at all?
- **Are they organized and logical?** If action plans are not logical or well organized, what implications does this have for their creators' future performance? What kind of work will these people produce once they are on your payroll?

> **A-Player Principle:** Making a bad hire is worse than not hiring anyone at all. Creating a stringent interview process minimizes your bad hiring decisions.

Passion Is Demonstrated by Preparation

You want to hire employees who have a career mentality rather than a nine-to-five mind-set. The best people have a passion for their work that goes beyond a paycheck. One way to measure something as intangible as passion in job candidates is to assess the amount of preparation they do for an interview.

Let's say that two candidates show up for an interview for a medical products sales position. One person has done some cursory research on the company using Google. The other candidate arrives with a detailed action plan to grow a new sales territory. This includes a map indicating the location of every doctor's office within a 30-mile radius of his home that could be a prospect. Which candidate seems more passionate about the role?

This is a true story, by the way. The candidate who came up with the MapQuest™-based plan had been trying to break into the medical products industry for years. He was passionate about the job and wanted it badly. This motivation showed up in his preparation. He got the job and is proving himself to be an A-player.

As Michael Vaughan, vice president of sales at TicketLeap, says, "I don't like hearing the question 'What do you do?' from a job candidate. I want to hire people who have taken the time to figure that out *before* they speak with me." Today, anyone with nominal initiative can research your company and come to an interview prepared to ask good questions. If you don't see at least that level of preparation, you have to question his or her passion for what you do.

A-Player Principle: The amount of preparation that candidates do before meeting with you helps you to gauge how much they want to work for you. You don't want to be a temporary parking space for an employee who has an eye on a different employment prize.

A-Player Payoff Points

Chapter 9: Interviewing and the Economic Power of Good Looks

- A-players are attracted by high standards. As long as it's logical, don't be afraid to use a vigorous interview process
  (*continued*)

(continued)

that screens out weak performers and challenges A-players to show their talents.

- Always define an A-Player Profile before you start interviewing. You have to know what makes people A-players in order to consistently select them during the interview process.
- Capture and quantify your A-Player Profile using validated personnel assessment tools. These tools help you to stay objective, weed out mediocre talent, and spot A-players.
- Use team interviews, multiple interviewers, and several days of interviews to catch important insights that a lone interviewer conducting one interview will miss.
- Ask candidates open-ended questions about their past accomplishments—and always ask follow-up questions. You will conduct an effective interview every time.
- Make sure that candidates know that you will call all of their previous supervisors as references. This encourages people to be honest with you about their weaknesses as well as their strengths.
- Look for opportunities to spend time with job candidates outside of your office. Changing the setting gives you the opportunity to learn more about people and how well they conduct themselves.
- Use live-fire exercises to see job candidates in action. Don't just rely on their answers to interview questions to make your hiring decision.
- Look for well-prepared candidates who have taken the time to learn about your industry and your company. A candidate's preparation is a good indicator of his or her passion for a career with your company.

Popping the Hood on Candidates Using Assessment Tools

Several years ago, I bought a used BMW 325 convertible. Before purchasing it, I reviewed at least 50 cars online and found the one that I wanted. The seller provided me with a Carfax® report indicating that it had never been in an accident. I had a friend test drive it before I flew to Dallas to pick up the car. Just to be safe, I took it to a local BMW dealer there to have it quickly looked over. The dealer gave it a clean bill of health. I wrote the check, got in the car, and drove it home. Life was good.

I took the car to a BMW specialist to fix a few small things once I was back. He opened the driver's-side door, took one look at the inside of the door panel, and said to me: "You know that this car has been in an accident, don't you?" No, I did not know that! "Absolutely," he said. "Look right here; you can see that the VIN number of the car doesn't appear on the inside of this door—but it *does* appear on the passenger side door. The driver's-side door is an aftermarket product. This door was replaced after an accident."

So much for my forensic abilities as a used car buyer. Fortunately, the car was great, and I enjoyed every moment of driving it. However, I learned my lesson: It is not enough to do a cursory check on a used car. You have to hire an expert to review every inch of it before you make a purchase. If nothing else, knowing that the car had been in an accident could have helped me cut an even better deal on the price.

Hiring people is like buying cars. Even with an in-depth interview process, it helps to have an expert "pop the hood" on candidates to see how much horsepower they have and to detect flaws that have gone unnoticed. The best personnel assessments provide this kind of insight. Implemented correctly, they help you to identify A-players and avoid hiring mistakes.

A-Player Principle: Use quality personnel assessment tools to pop the hood on job candidates and get quick, accurate insights on the strengths and weaknesses of the people you interview.

Solving the People Puzzle

The other day, I was talking with the vice president of sales for a commercial flooring company about integrating online assessment tools into his hiring process. He was excited about the idea and told me that he was going to have his best salesperson take the assessment as a trial. When I reviewed the salesperson's results, I knew right away that there was a problem. The assessment described an account manager who was brought in *after* the sale, not a "hunter" responsible for bringing in new business.

I have learned after years of doing this kind of work that you have to trust the assessment results. So I e-mailed the results to the executive, called him to follow up, and gave him my interpretation. There was a pause on the other end of the line. Then he said to me, "Well, I will admit it. I was testing you. I didn't assess my top sales guy. I assessed the guy who *should* be my top sales guy. He is polished, professional, smart, and clients love him; but he can't generate new business. He is an enigma." It took me just five minutes to show this executive how the assessment report clearly revealed why this salesperson didn't generate much new business. How valuable would this information have proved before hiring this person?

The people we hire can puzzle us. The ones who appear to have great abilities can fall short, while others who are not at the top of our lists end up being superb performers. How can you tell which is which? Good assessment tools can help by shedding light on people's hidden gifts and flaws *before* you hire them. Specifically, these tools help you to:

- Identify the skills and talents that are critical for top performance.
- Measure the skills and talents of the people you interview.
- Compare the abilities of candidates to an A-Player Profile.
- Analyze the gaps between what the job requires and the talents people bring to the table.

By "personnel assessments," I'm referring to online tests that provide feedback on job candidates' skills and abilities. These tools measure talents that are difficult to teach, such as sales effectiveness, leadership ability, competitiveness, sense of urgency, analytical orientation, personal motivation, and practical thinking. They also provide insight into critical but intangible factors like a person's intuitiveness about others, self-confidence, "coachability," and drive to achieve.

If potential employees don't bring the right combination of skills and abilities with them to a position, their chances of failure increase dramatically. By using assessment tools to make sure that all your final candidates have these foundational aptitudes, you're able to focus on finding the A-players among the candidates that you interview. Good evaluation instruments provide you with insight into people that you can't get otherwise.

Assessment tools provide an additional benefit. They temper your natural tendency to be charmed by certain candidates and pursue them despite their weaknesses. I know seasoned sales executives who refuse to interview any potential salespeople until they have completed an online sales assessment. These executives have made too many hiring mistakes based solely on initial impressions and "gut instincts." They like the fact that assessment tools inject objectivity about candidates into the interview process.

> **A-Player Principle:** We like to like people and to be liked in return. Assessment tools help us remain objective about the people that we interview.

Creating a Common Language

Evaluation tools like these also give you a common language to use in your organization as you interview, assess, and discuss candidates. Executives in sales organizations, for instance, will buy into the importance of measuring competitiveness, energy, money motivation, and drive to achieve—all of which are specific categories measured by sales assessment instruments. This common language helps multiple interviewers to evaluate numerous candidates quickly.

Avoid Hiring Landmines

Translating your A-Player Profile into an assessment benchmark and then evaluating candidates against these criteria help you to avoid hiring landmines.

For example, executives often learn an industry while working for a big company and then take a leadership role with a smaller company in the same industry. They try to reproduce their success by hiring exactly the same people they used to hire at the old place. The problem with this approach is that different companies have different A-Player Profiles and require distinct types of employees. If you came to a small company from a much bigger organization, the titles used may be identical, but the actual requirements of these roles are often very different. People in smaller organizations typically are expected to wear multiple hats and handle a broader range of responsibilities than they do in larger enterprises. Salespeople have more account management responsibilities; operational employees have more direct client contact; executives have to roll up their sleeves and get more involved in tactical issues. You must take these changes into account when you are hiring—or you greatly increase the chances of a hiring mistake. Assessing candidates based on the right A-Player Profile gives you consistent, impartial data with which to make good hiring decisions.

> **A-Player Principle:** Always assess the job for which you are hiring before you assess people for the job. If you don't understand what the job requires, it's impossible to determine if someone is right for the role.

Revealing the Gaps between People and Positions

Good assessment tools allow you to see how well an individual's profile fits with a job's requirements. Someone who has an ideal sales profile typically won't last a month in a project management role. The best project managers, conversely, often fail miserably in sales roles. Strong personnel assessments highlight the gaps between the skills a job requires and the skills a candidate possesses. The bigger the gaps, the larger the likelihood that the candidate won't do the job well.

The Sweet-and-Sour Effect

I know a woman who is a top salesperson for a company in the kitchen and bath industry. She is hard-charging and fast-paced. Yet she also has incredibly strong practical thinking and problem-solving skills. On a 10-point scale, she has an unusually high score of 9. This combination of two seemingly unrelated talents—what I call the sweet-and-sour effect—makes this woman a superb performer. She can quickly solve construction and remodeling problems *and* effectively sell the solutions that she creates.

We therefore always look for individuals who possess this combination of skills when we assess salespeople for this particular company. When we find someone who has them, we quickly schedule an interview. If all goes well, the company moves swiftly to hire the person because it knows how difficult it is to find salespeople with this combination of abilities.

Alternatively, in design-related fields, if you hire anyone who has low practical thinking scores, watch out. I have worked for years with architectural and design firms to build and lead A-player teams. I have learned that a lack of practical thinking skills severely limits architects' ability to move up the professional food chain. Rather than pouring a lot of time and money into coaching people who lack these skills, it's best to screen them out in the interview process and instead hire people who have better talents. Good

A-Player Principle: A-players often have a unique combination of skills that helps them to excel. Assessment tools can quickly reveal if people possess these abilities.

assessment instruments are invaluable in uncovering these kinds of weaknesses early—*before* they cost you a lot of money.

Who Will Be Motivated to Do the Job?

Whether people have the skills to do a job or not, they will not be long-term successes if they lack the appropriate motivation for a role. In contrast, a great motivational profile can turn a borderline candidate into an A-player. I once assessed a salesperson named Brian whose profile was not ideal for an outside sales role. He was less assertive and more analytical than many top salespeople, a profile that could hinder him from effectively prospecting for new business. However, he was strongly motivated by money but still concerned with serving people. He was also motivated just enough by independence and autonomy to thrive in a position that required a lot of self-direction. Yet he was not *so* autonomous that he rebelled against the authority structure of this sales organization. He also had extremely high scores in understanding people, practical thinking, and personal drive.

When you looked at Brian's overall profile and took into account his solid sales experience (he had a record of accomplishment selling office equipment), you saw an A-player. Sure enough, he has become one of the company's top producers.

Compare this to Janet, a sales candidate I assessed for another wholesaler. This woman had a perfect sales profile in the sense that she was assertive, outgoing, fast-paced, and didn't get bogged down in details. She, like Brian, had very high personal effectiveness scores. However, her motivational profile was the *exact* opposite of the ideal for the position. She was not motivated by making money.

> **A-Player Principle:** People can have all the skills in the world, but if they lack the right motivators, they won't stick around. Assessment tools let you assess if a job candidate is motivated by what your position has to offer.

The wholesaler hired her and saw her excel as a sales rep, but only for a time. Ultimately, Janet was not driven enough by the financial rewards of the job to stay with the company. She ended up leaving to spend more time with her kids and to pursue other interests that paid less but that she found more rewarding.

Avoiding an Organ Rejection: The Importance of Cultural Fit

The topic of cultural fit often comes up when I consult with companies. Every executive understands on a gut level that A-players typically possess more than just strong technical skills. A-players also build relationships, earn trust, and influence others in ways that make the entire organization more effective. Zeroing in on such skills is another area where the right assessment tools can help to avoid bad hires.

I once aided a consulting firm in improving its business development and client satisfaction results. As part of this project, we assessed every consultant from the managing partners to entry-level associates. One particular item jumped out at me upon reviewing the results: Not one person in this entire firm was deeply motivated by personal autonomy and having control. In fact, most of the consultants disliked people who wanted to be in the limelight. This firm's leaders supported a highly democratic environment in which no one felt left out or taken advantage of as decisions were made.

Anyone strongly motivated by autonomy and control would stick out in this firm. Their coworkers would dislike them and see them as power-hungry and constantly jockeying for position. Like a body rejecting a transplanted organ, this firm was likely to snub any individual who did not fit into its democratic culture.

Of course, there could be a situation where this firm actually *needed* to hire a much more autonomous, individualistic person for a particular role. But because of this cultural issue, the firm's leaders needed to pay special attention to the motivational profile of everyone hired. We used assessment tools to identify people with both the technical skills and the cultural fit to be effective in this environment.

> **A-Player Principle:** New employees can have all the right skills yet flounder because they don't fit well with your corporate culture. Assessment tools can help you to spot cultural misfits during the hiring process.

Are People Driven to Achieve?

The president of a payroll company contacted me recently with a request to evaluate one of his salespeople. The results came back almost picture perfect. You could have framed this profile and used it as an example of a strong outside sales rep. However, there was one major hole. This person was totally unmotivated to achieve. The assessments revealed that he was frustrated with his job, his goals for the future were unclear, and he had a negative attitude. His lack of motivation showed up in his sales activity. He focused too much on analysis and planning and neglected the need to prospect for new clients.

The president immediately took these results and challenged the salesperson with them. The jury is still out on whether the salesperson is going to make it. However, there's a lesson to be learned here before you hire a new salesperson or any other employee: Insight into people's motivation and drive is invaluable. Someone with terrific skills but no drive to achieve is not going to be an A-player. The ideal candidate for *any* position possesses both past accomplishments and the motivation to achieve in the future. The lack of either one of these key factors is a yellow flag that must be addressed in the interview process.

The Difference between Drive and Self-Esteem

In my experience, the best job candidates often have good self-esteem, but they are *always* driven to achieve. Despite their seeming similarities, these are two very different qualities. A top salesperson with whom I work has poor self-esteem as measured by assessment tools. However, he likes his job, has strong sales skills, and has clear goals that he is motivated to achieve. His performance qualifies him as an A-player in every sense.

Conversely, I have assessed poor performers whose self-esteem levels were through the roof. Their problem was that they felt they had "arrived." They were not motivated to achieve because they were satisfied with their current circumstances. This perspective is often not accurate. (Many people who think they have arrived actually never departed.) But this lack of drive can be hard to detect in an interview. Good assessment tools can help to reveal this hidden problem and keep you from hiring someone you shouldn't.

> **A-Player Principle:** There is a difference between drive and self-esteem. A-players may or may not have high self-esteem, but they are always motivated to achieve.

Integrating Assessments into the Interview Process

Now that you understand the value that good assessment tools bring to hiring A-players, here are eight key steps of the interview process with information on where and how to integrate these tools.

1. **Identify candidates**. You initially recruit potential A-players from referrals, online applications, or a recruiter.
2. **Review the resumes**. Do individuals have the basic background, experience, and accomplishments for which you are looking? Do they match your A-Player Profile?
3. **Initial screen**. Schedule and conduct an initial phone screen. Confirm skills and experiences. Do candidates make the initial cut? Are they worth bringing in for a face-to-face interview?
4. **First interview and online assessment**. Some companies conduct first interviews and then assess the candidates in whom

they are interested. Others require that people complete an assessment before they are interviewed. In either case, use these evaluations early in the process in order to factor the results into the following round of interviews.

5. **Review interview and assessment results**. What came out of the first interview? How do people's accomplishments match up with the job? How do the assessment results match up with the position's requirements? What strengths speak for candidates? What weaknesses speak against them?

6. **Invite candidates back for second interviews**. Weed out weaker people and invite the rest back for second interviews. Include questions that are based on the assessment results. Dig into potential weaknesses. Look for good cultural fit.

7. **Check** references, complete background and drug tests as required.

8. **Identify** your top candidates, make employment offers, and get them started.

Proven Tips for Using Assessments Effectively

Here are some additional tips for using assessment tools to avoid hiring mistakes as part of your interview and hiring process.

Bring Job Candidates into Your Office to Complete Pre-Employment Assessments

While most online assessments are accessed via an easily e-mailed password, have job candidates come into your office to complete these evaluations if possible. This is the only way you can verify that the person you are interviewing in New York—not her superstar sales rep cousin in California—actually answers the assessment questions.

Assess Early in the Interview Process

Have candidates complete an assessment as soon as you decide that they are contenders for a position. Sometimes this means that you interview them face to face first. In other situations, they can undergo these appraisals before you ever meet them. I have found that having the assessment reports in hand helps executives to overcome personal bias that often rears its head during the interview process.

For example, I recently assessed a salesperson for a financial services company who does not make the best first impression when you meet him. You question whether he has the polish and professionalism to succeed in this industry. However, his assessment results reveal an A-player sales profile. Without these results, an employer may well have cut him after the first interview—and lost an A-player. With these assessment results in hand, interviewers are more likely to bring him in for a second interview. (By the way, even with a lack of polish, this sales representative is generating fantastic results for his employer.)

Find Assessments That Work and Trust Them

Take the time to find assessment instruments that work. Make sure that your assessment provider explains the results to you in plain English, not psycho-babble. Confirm that executives and managers who oversee hiring for you understand the assessments and the insight they provide.

Then trust the assessments. If an assessment tool shows a candidate to have great strengths, act quickly to interview the person and hire him or her if you remain impressed. If the assessment results reveal danger signs, then take that seriously too. Follow up on those issues in the interview process. Dig in to see if and how these weaknesses show up in the candidate's professional track record.

One of my clients is a large advertising and promotional agency whose controller was interviewing accountants for his department. We included an online assessment benchmark and candidate appraisal in the interview process. One of the candidates had a terrific personality and interviewed very well. However, her assessment results indicated that she lacked the ability to diagnose problems and to focus on analytical issues—which were key abilities required by this role.

Based on this feedback, the controller and his team dug into her past accomplishments in diagnosing, analyzing, and fixing technical accounting problems. It turned out that this woman did not have nearly as much hands-on experience in these areas as they had thought. In fact, her former teammates had taken care of these issues. As a result, my client eliminated her from consideration. Had it not been for the assessment results, they likely would have missed these weaknesses and made a poor and costly hiring decision.

Background Checks and Drug Tests

The focus of this chapter is on assessments that dig into a candidate's talents and skills. Another set of valuable tools checks the personal backgrounds of job candidates and screens for illegal drug use. You should consult your attorney on if and how these tools apply to your company and the positions for which you are hiring. It's generally a good idea to use these kinds of tests, for two reasons.

- They help you to catch additional job-related factors that are vital to consider in the hiring process. For instance, a criminal background check is a must if you employ technicians who work in customers' homes.
- Including these tests in your hiring process deters people with problems in these areas from applying in the first place. However, some people who know they won't pass these tests will still apply on the hope that they will slip through. There are many providers of these types of tests. Get referrals and verify the quality as well as the prices of the services you consider.

Legal Compliance

Many people have questions about the legal issues associated with using personnel assessment instruments. These tools must test job candidates against job-related factors and cannot be biased against particular groups. Your assessment provider should be able to give you documentation indicating that its assessments comply with the Equal Employment Opportunity Commission's requirements. The U.S. Department of Labor Employment and Training Administration provides an online report entitled *Testing and Assessment: An Employer's Guide to Good Practices* that provides good guidance on establishing an effective assessment process in your company. http://wdr.doleta.gov/opr/fulltext/document.cfm?docn=6032

A-Player Payoff Points

Chapter 10: Popping the Hood on Candidates Using Assessment Tools

- Good assessment tools help you to pop the hood on job candidates and evaluate their strengths and weaknesses relative to a position's requirements.
- You will make serious and costly mistakes if you rely too much on first impressions and gut feel when hiring. Assessment tools help you to check your emotional reactions to people with more objective data.
- Companies often hire the wrong person because they have not accurately defined the A-Player Profile for a position. The right assessment tools capture and quantify this Profile so you can compare job candidates to it.
- A-players often have a unique combination of skills that average performers lack. Assessment tools help you to pinpoint these skills and watch for them in every person that you interview.
- People can have all the skills in the world, but they will not succeed if they lack the right motivation. Use assessment tools to determine if people are motivated by the rewards that your company and position have to offer them.
- Every company wants to hire people who fit well into its culture. The right assessment tools help you to identify potential cultural misfits before you hire them.
- There is no replacement for personal drive and ambition. Using assessment tools helps you to see if people are willing to pay the cost required to be successful.

Conclusion: Keeping the A-Players You Hire

Recruiting A-players is not a second-class business problem that we delegate to human resources because we can't be bothered with it. It is a sustainable, competitive advantage that can move our company ahead of our competitors and help to keep it there. Remember, C-players don't typically become A-players, so you have to build a system for finding A-players. You can't simply accept the hand that has been dealt to you. Just one A-player—and certainly a handful of them—can transform almost any business.

While it's vital to *find* A-players, this won't be enough to take your company to the next level. You also must *keep* the A-players you hire—which means that you have to be an effective leader and coach.

I wrote this book in part because we waste so much time coaching people who can't rise to the challenges before them. When we hire A-players, we acquire people who can make big contributions and achieve significant goals. However, A-players have more career options than do weaker performers. We must therefore make it worth their while to stay employed with us. You want to build a great company. What's in it for your A-players? You need to have an answer for that question, or else they will go to work for someone who does.

A-Players Want to Work for Strong Leaders

A-players want to work for a leader who has a vision for the business and can tell them where they as top performers fit into it. A sales rep who works for a fast-growing distribution company told me the story of how her organization relocated warehouse space to a bigger facility nearby. The chief executive enlisted every employee to help move all the inventory from the old warehouse into the new one. By Saturday afternoon, the move was completed, and the company was ready for business to open on Monday morning without missing a beat. The CEO broke out a few beers for the crew and gave a toast to a great period of growth that necessitated more warehouse space. The sales rep went up to the CEO afterward and congratulated him on having brought this vision of a new warehouse into reality. He smiled and said, "I'll probably get two good nights of sleep and then I will start worrying about where our new warehouse should be. We'll outgrow this one in less than three years."

The sales rep was amazed. She was thinking about serving customers *today*, not the moves required to support the company's growth three years from now. This CEO, on the other hand, had a vision for his warehouse needs three years hence. He also knew how many sales representatives he would need to support this kind of growth, which current salespeople could become managers for new sales teams, which members of his distribution team could lead an operation twice the current size, and where the holes in his team lay. A-players thrive under this kind of forward thinking.

It's easy to become so embroiled in the details of running your business that you don't step back and figure out how to create a team that can turn your vision into reality. Let's take a look at some specific steps you can take to cultivate this kind of thinking and use it to keep your A-players engaged and motivated.

A-Player Principle: A-players want to work for leaders who know where they as top performers fit in the future of the business. Time invested in clarifying and communicating your vision pays off by helping to keep the A-players that you hire.

Define Your Organizational Strategy —————

To keep your A-players, you need an organizational strategy. As I touched on briefly in Chapter 1, a simple and surprisingly effective tool in this regard is an organizational chart. Start with the business goals that you want to achieve. What does success look like for your business? Then create the right organizational chart to achieve these objectives. What are the key results for each role? How do these connect to your larger business goals? Trust me, clarity in this area goes a long way. If you take the time to clarify your goals and sketch out the right organization to achieve them, you will be ahead of many businesses.

Once you complete this chart, you're ready to start writing in the names of your current team members. This is a great process because it's a quick gap analysis of the team that you have versus the team that you need. Here's what you are likely to find:

- You'll have a few people (the A-players) whose names are easy to write in. In fact, you could write them into almost any box in that chart.
- You will also have some people who can become A-players if you help them get up to speed.
- You'll also have folks who can be valuable, but in a more limited capacity.
- Finally, you have employees (C-players and below) who don't belong in your organization at all.

> **A-Player Principle:** An organizational chart is a quick and effective tool to analyze the strengths, weaknesses, opportunities, and threats inherent in your current team.

If these descriptions line up reasonably well with your organization, what do you do with each of these groups? Here are some steps to follow.

1. **Invest your time with your A-players first.** You have to make sure that your A-players understand their roles and futures with your company. Give them plenty of responsibility, and bring them into your inner circle of leaders and confidants. Schedule a regular meeting with these people (weekly, biweekly, or monthly depending on the situation). Remember: Time invested with your A-players yields a big payoff. Don't neglect these people because you have too many other problems to deal with. *They are the solution.*

2. **Provide your B-players with coaching and accountability.** Many times, your B-players are within shouting distance of being A-players and just need some nudging to get there. Help them focus on the right activities. Ask them to take their game to the next level. Schedule regular meetings where you or a manager coach them, work with them to set goals, and provide accountability.

3. **Turn some borderline performers into A-players by scaling down their roles.** Some B-players can become A-players when you reduce their responsibilities to fit their aptitudes. Don't apologize for getting these people focused on a smaller set of duties. Instead, challenge them to become "black belts" in the areas where they are talented.

4. **Replace C-players and below with people from your farm team**—particularly if you have tried your best to lead and coach them to a better level of performance. These performance problems will not go away. After reading this book, you should have a farm team from which to call up a new player. The good news is that now you have the right people to put into this role. The bad news is that you no longer have an excuse. It's time to make a change.

A-Player Principle: First invest time with your A-players, and then spend time with everyone else. A-players contribute the most to your success *and* set a fast pace for everyone else on your team.

Be Objective and Make the Time

You need two things to implement your organizational strategy: objectivity and time. Objectivity means that you must remove yourself emotionally from your current team in order to design the organizational structure that you need. Carving out time is also critical, because this kind of exercise is very important but rarely urgent. Other tasks will always try to push this work aside. You must make it a priority. The payoffs from it are potentially huge.

Because of both these factors, you should consider hiring a consultant or some other trusted advisor who really understands this process to help you through it. This person should provide you with a strategic framework, help you to define the organizational structure, offer guidance based on experience doing similar projects for other companies, and provide ongoing advice and accountability. It's worth spending money with a good person to have this done well.

Completing this work allows you to provide your A-players with the clarity and focus they need to step up and contribute more to your business. By defining people's roles and giving them focus, your employees—particularly your A-players—quickly take more ownership, responsibility, and initiative. Watching your key people embrace your business is enough to make this whole exercise worth the effort.

I recently spoke with a business owner about the strategic importance of having an organizational chart for a business. He told me that he agreed completely and then showed me the one he had developed for his company. I took a look at it and asked him, "Why isn't there a financial role on this chart?" He looked at me and said, "That's not necessary—I handle all the finances."

He had completely missed the point of revisiting your organizational chart: to help you *remove yourself* from the business while creating an overview of every role required for profitably acquiring, serving, and keeping customers. You define the roles needed to make your business run *apart* from the people you currently employ—and that includes yourself. As Michael Gerber points out in his legendary business book *The E-Myth*, a good organizational chart is meant to focus you on hiring the right people to fill more and more of the tactical roles in your organization. This frees you up to focus on the strategic roles where you add the most value.[1]

> **A-Player Principle:** Good intentions are not enough. Hire a trusted advisor to help you implement the strategies in this book.

A Close Look at Your Organizational Chart

We all know what a basic organizational chart looks like, but here are five steps to follow in putting this together for your company or your team.

1. **Define the roles that need to be filled.** These might include president and vice presidents of finance, marketing, sales, operations, and so on for an entire business. For a team within a business, the roles might be sales manager, sales representatives, and sales support or other appropriate titles.
2. **Define key results for each role.** What does success look like for each role on this chart? How would you know if someone performed this job terrifically well?
3. **Define responsibilities.** What do the people in these roles have to do in order to achieve the key results just listed?
4. **Define measurements.** How should people keep score in this role? How can they measure their own progress and determine if they are on track?
5. **Define value.** How much money can the company potentially make or save if this role is performed well?

Coaching and Keeping A-Players

I know a financial analyst who recently received the highest performance review of anyone in her 400-person department. In fact, she was the only person in the entire department to receive a "superior" rating. While this was great for this individual, it was not a good sign for the company. When only one person out of 400 receives a superior rating, you have a department filled with B and C-players who are content with the status quo . . . and one A-player who wonders if her future lies with this company. The department had obviously not emphasized hiring A-players. If you're this person's boss, you had better start talking about an advancement plan for her as soon as you deliver this rating. If you don't, you will lose her. Take immediate steps to coach and keep your A-players.

I Was Thinking about You

Some of the most powerful words that you can say to an A-player are "I was thinking about you." As I have said, typically we waste too much time trying to get C-players to improve instead of investing more time with our A-players. When was the last time you spoke one-on-one with your A-players about their careers? A-players are typically ambitious and want to move to the next level. You risk losing them if they don't see a clear path for advancement at your company.

Go back to your organizational chart. Where have you written the names of your A-players? How do you envision their roles one year from now? Three years from now? Clarify your thoughts, then pull each A-player aside and say, "I was thinking about you. Let's grab some lunch and talk about your career and what's next for you." People want to know that their boss is thinking about them and their future.

Go to these meetings prepared to discuss your ideas. You don't have to make up some fancy document. Just pull out a legal pad and sketch things out. By and large, I have found that people are terrible at setting goals with a "clean sheet of paper." Most people want help clarifying objectives for their careers. By providing thoughtful guidance, you focus your employees on objectives that are valuable to them and to your business. You abdicate leadership responsibility when you ask people, "What do you want to do next in your career?" without having some ideas for them. If people are good, they deserve some of your mind time to help them manage their careers effectively.

At the same time, let them know that your ideas are not set in concrete. Invite them to talk about what they want to achieve and get their input. Take the opportunity to hear their perspective on what is working at the company and what could be better. Incorporate what you hear into these plans.

Finally, commit to concrete next steps for turning this plan into reality. This includes giving them the opportunity to make more money. While most people are not primarily motivated by money, as a friend of mine says, "Money doesn't talk. It screams." If you have A-players who are making valuable contributions to your business, provide them with raises that are commensurate with their contributions.

You can go a long way toward locking in an A-player by following these steps. Of course, there are no guarantees in life. People make career changes for all kinds of reasons. But when you take this approach, you're doing everything that you can to ensure that your A-players stay engaged in building your business.

Most A-players are strongly motivated by the idea of moving to the next level in their careers and lives. They want to make progress. They don't want their job to be a gerbil wheel that calls for massive expenditures of energy while going . . . nowhere. Stay ahead of your A-players when it comes to where and how they fit into your company's future. And be sure to deliver on your promises. Give them bigger challenges, more responsibility, and more money right away. Then keep all three coming as fast as people can handle them.

> **A-Player Principle:** A-players don't want to be taken for granted. Make sure they know where they fit in the future of your business.

Look to the Future

Your company must be great at recruiting A-players if you're going to have the talent necessary to fuel growth and drive profits. If you have a vision for a world-class company, then improving the recruiting function at your company is a priority—and it's time to get on it. However, when you don't have a big recruiting department, you need smart, cost-effective strategies for finding and hiring A-players. I hope that this book has provided these to you and spurred you on to pursue the vision of creating the business you want by creating the team of A-players you need.

My prediction is that recruiting will become one of the most important corporate initiatives that we as businesspeople discuss over the next decade. Increasingly, the media is going to pick up on what you already know: No matter the state of the economy, it's never easy to find A-player employees. The companies that build systems for hiring and keeping A-players are going to beat their competitors.

Take this to heart. Treat recruiting like every other critical business function. Build a system to accomplish your goals and hire strong people to work the system. Provide your company with the talent for which it hungers. Stay ahead of your A-players, and keep them engaged in building your business. If you implement these strategies, while others may know the secret, you will be *acting* on it. Leaders who create great companies never do it alone. They always create a team of A-players.

Web Sites for Free Additional Resources

Visit www.howtohireaplayers.com for free resources to help you build your own A-player team, including checklists, templates, additional advice, further articles, assessment materials, and more.

Visit www.herrenkohlconsulting.com for video clips and other information about Eric Herrenkohl's consulting, coaching, writing, and professional speaking.

Notes

Chapter 1

1. "The Search for Talent," *The Economist*, October 7, 2006, 22.
2. William (Lord Kelvin) Thomson, *Constitution of Matter*. Vol. 1 of *Popular Lectures and Addresses* (London: Richard Clay and Sons, 1891), 80.
3. Michael Gerber, *The E-Myth Revisited* (New York: HarperCollins, 1986), 105.

Chapter 3

1. "401 Players Taken before Pujols in '99," *San Diego Union Tribune*, October 26, 2004.
2. "Another Difficulty for a Microsoft-Yahoo Marriage: Recruiting," *New York Times*, February 4, 2008.

Chapter 4

1. Public Broadcasting System, *American Experience: The Kennedys,* air date May 2009.

Chapter 5

1. Robert Caro, *Master of the Senate* (New York: Random House, 2002), 106.

Chapter 6

1. U.S. Census Bureau News Press Release, February 25, 2009, "As Baby Boomers Age, Fewer Families Have Children Under 18 at Home." www.census.gov/Press-Release/www/releases/archives/families _house holds/013378.html

Chapter 9

1. Kate Lorenz, "Do Pretty People Earn More?" CNN.com, July 8, 2005.
2. Bradford D. Smart, *Topgrading* (New York: Penguin Group, 2005), 325.

Conclusion

1. Michael Gerber, *The E-Myth* (New York: HarperCollins, 1986), 100.

Index